The MIDPOINT

How to Write the Central Turning Point with Emotion, Tension, & Depth

Mary Lynn Mercer

The Midpoint: How to Write the Central Turning Point with Emotion, Tension, & Depth

First print edition, May 2014
ISBN: 0-692-23862-X
ISBN-13: 978-0-692-23862-2

Red bow on cover: Elena Schweitzer / Shutterstock. Swamp background: Memo Angeles / Shutterstock. Red firecrackers: Jiang Hongyan / Shutterstock. Fireworks display setup at night: Fer Gregory / Shutterstock. Red fireworks explosions: Arie v.d. Wolde / Shutterstock. Eye icon: Wiktoria Pawlak / Shutterstock. Road barrier icon: kontur-vid / Shutterstock. Cartoon character with trap: 3drenderings / Shutterstock. Alligator: Petrovic Igor / Shutterstock. Magnifying glass: Marish / Shutterstock. Handshake heart: Denis Maliugin / Shutterstock. Firefighting icon: Kapreski / Shutterstock. Dog: Ovchynnikov Oleksii / Shutterstock. Bomb: DoodleDance / Shutterstock. Used under license.

Book cover design by: Mary L. Mercer 2014

"Port Credit" font by Ray Larabie. "Futura" font by Paul Renner. "Antonio" font by Vernon Adams. "Avenir" and "Avenir Next Condensed" fonts by Adrian Frutiger. "Simonetta" font by Brownfox. "Vollkorn" font by Friedrich Althausen. Used under license.

About the Author

Mary Lynn Mercer's first nonfiction book, *Story Bones: How to X-Ray Any Novel for Plot, Conflict, and Character,* hit #1 on Amazon's Kindle Screenwriting bestsellers list the first week of release. An experienced national contest judge, avid reader, and movie buff, she enjoys applying creative tools gleaned from years of study and pleasure reading to her own writing. For information on other and future releases, please visit her website at *MaryMercer.weebly.com.*

ALSO BY MARY L. MERCER:

Story Bones: How to X-Ray Any Novel for Plot, Conflict, and Character

Standout Characters: How to Forge an Emotional Bond with Readers

The MIDPOINT

PRAISE FOR *STORY BONES:*

"One of the best crafting books I've ever read. What a fantastic book! I love it! Everybody needs to check out Mary's book ASAP."
– Carol A. Hughes, writer/director/producer, creator of the *Deep Story* writing method

For Mom

Table of Contents

The Great Swampy Middle 1
Character Flaws 5
Structure 15
Creating Tension 27
First Half of the Midpoint 41
"Quick Look" at the Glimpse 45
Glimpse 47
"Quick Look" at the Double Glimpse 59
Double Glimpse 61
"Quick Look" at the Cut Off 71
Cut Off 73
"Quick Look" at the Trap 81
Trap 83
"Quick Look" at the (1st Half) Attack 91
(1st Half) Attack 93
Mix and Match – Part 1 101
Second Half of the Midpoint 109
"Quick Look" at the Q & A 113
Questions & Answers 115
"Quick Look" at the Love vs. Goal 125
Love vs. Goal 127
"Quick Look" at the Escape 137
Escape 139
"Quick Look" at the (2nd Half) Attack 149
(2nd Half) Attack 151
Mix and Match – Part 2 161
Tools for Crafting Midpoint Beats 169

Midpoint Beats Chart ____ 184 - 185
Additional Examples from Novels, TV, & Movies ____ 187
Conclusion ____ 197
Texts Cited ____ 199

The Great Swampy Middle

Every fiction writer, regardless of experience, encounters it with every story they write. Plotter or pantser makes no difference. Once pen touches paper or fingers touch keyboard, it's only a matter of time. Before writing "The End" the unavoidable must be dealt with.

Best-selling fantasy author Jim Butcher calls it the Great Swampy Middle. "The middle of a book is *dangerous*," he says, noting that one wrong turn can cause a story to wander into water teaming with alligators and snakes that can kill it dead.

Memo Angeles / Shutterstock

Despite the Everglades-like perils of the middle, there is a simple way to safely navigate it and reach an ending satisfying to readers. Just as Theseus used Ariadne's thread to escape the same labyrinth that had defeated countless men and women before him, there exists a bright lifeline to rescue writers perishing in the Great Swampy Middle.

It's the Midpoint, and as the name suggests it occurs at exactly the halfway mark in the story.

Christopher Vogler in *The Writer's Journey, Second Edition* says it's "a major nerve ganglion of the story. Many threads of the hero's history lead in, and many threads of possibility and change lead out the other side." (160) The Midpoint is a big bow in the middle tying the story threads securely together.

How does mastering the Midpoint help writers survive and even thrive in the Everglades of the middle? Figuring out this central turning point guides a writer in sidestepping all kinds of quicksand. Dan Decker explains in *Anatomy of a Screenplay* that if a storytelling problem emerges, the cause is often buried much earlier in the story, because it takes time for developments in plot, conflict, and characterization to have their desired effect. As much as 25% of the story may go by before the reader begins to catch on that something's not working and feel dissatisfied. (159-160)

Now reverse-engineer Decker's rule of thumb and examine it from a positive perspective. Writing toward a strongly-crafted Midpoint will make character and plot decisions in the first half of the story more surefooted, and conflict in the second half of the story active and better-developed. The benefits are no sagging scenes, and a rising sense of anticipation in the writer for what comes next.

How does the Midpoint intensify readers' satisfaction? Most readers may not even know or care about dramatic structure, but they instinctively wait for something big to happen in the middle and follow the reverberations throughout the rest of the story. The Midpoint controls pace and tension, pulling deliciously taut all the story threads coming and going. It's responsible for keeping the reader happily turning pages to find out, "What happens next?" until they hit that spot in the middle where everything changes with a *bang!* Then they turn the pages even faster because they didn't expect *that* to happen.

Besides benefitting writers and readers, the Midpoint gives a huge boost to characters' internal growth. It's safe to say that an underdeveloped Midpoint marks a gaping hole in the protagonist's character arc. That's because the Midpoint empowers the character to recognize the need for internal change. It places an urgent demand upon him to decide for or against the thematic premise. Vice or virtue? Fear or faith? Flaw or strength? Which is it going to be?

The Midpoint is more than a "plot point," which erroneously suggests it's only about plot. Nevertheless, it does impact the plot in a big way. Plot is created from a motivated character overcoming strong conflict in pursuit of a tangible goal. The Midpoint simultaneously jerks the slack out of each one of those elements. It challenges and intensifies the protagonist's motivation. It reveals the conflict is a lot stronger than he bargained for. And it demands he either change up his goal or the way he's been going after it.

Tying story threads together also means the Midpoint is where external conflict and internal conflict powerfully collide. The protagonist and antagonist confront each other here over high stakes (consequences) regarding the external plot. Sparks from their external confrontation sets a new awareness burning brightly in the protagonist, forcing him to decide between opposing internal values. He still wants his goal, but is he willing to give up his flaw in order to get it?

So slip on your waders, slap on your Indiana Jones-style fedora, and follow the scarlet cord of the Midpoint safely past snapping gators and hissing moccasins. Revive a sense of enthusiasm for your story and never get lost in the Great Swampy Middle again.

Character Flaws

The Florida swamp known as the Everglades is actually a very wide and slow-moving river. Similarly, pulsing beneath the surface of the Great Swampy Middle flows an undercurrent that subtly yet inexorably commands the direction of the entire story.

That force is the protagonist's flaw.

While the protagonist needs certain skills and strengths in order to have a hope, however slim and tenuous, of success, he also needs weaknesses. Flaws not only help make characters appealing by saving them from unrealistic Barbie Doll perfection, but also rescue them from being reactive victims.

It's a fact of the fallen human condition that no one is perfect. Romans 3:23 says, "For all have sinned, and come short of the glory of God." An essential component of developing three-dimensional characters is to give each one a set of shortcomings or weaknesses that hamper their success or happiness.

One strength that every protagonist lacks at the beginning of the story is self-awareness. He's his own worst enemy, but doesn't have a clue. If he knew, then the story would be over. Lesson learned. Instead, it's the story's job to put him through a world of physical and emotional hurt until revelation dawns bright and clear, usually near the end. But between the beginning and that bright dawn of enlightenment lies the Great Swampy Middle, where flaws are tested, stretched, and hammered until finally broken.

The protagonist's flaw sets the parameters for the entire story. Beyond marking the end, it pulls the trigger on the starting gun at the beginning. John Truby in *The Anatomy of Story* says the opening problem "should be an outside manifestation of the hero's weakness." (42)

In the romantic comedy *While You Were Sleeping* (1995), Lucy's (Sandra Bullock) problem at the beginning of the story is she's mistaken by a distraught family for their comatose son's fiancee. She's not a naturally dishonest person, but nevertheless finds herself caught up in a snowballing lie of life-altering proportions.

So how did she get into this fix? Lucy's flaw at the beginning of the story is she fantasizes about life instead of taking action to grab hold of happiness. She daydreams constantly about marrying a certain handsome stranger she's seen but never actually met. At the hospital her flaw, however unintentionally, directly triggers the misunderstandings that kick off the story when she's overheard telling herself, "I was going to marry him."

The protagonist's flaw directly contributes and shapes the opening problem, but does he recognize or acknowledge his part in this crisis? Remember that at the beginning self-awareness is in short supply. Though the protagonist is facing the external manifestation of his defining weakness, he clings to denial. He doesn't yet recognize the hindrance his flaw represents to his goal or essential relationships. In *While You Were Sleeping,* Lucy blames the nurse for not recognizing she was merely talking to herself.

By denying any personal responsibility for the opening problem, the protagonist holds tightly to his flaw. Why does he want to continue hanging onto something that just landed him in the biggest trouble he's ever faced in his life?

Rob Tobin in *The Screenwriting Formula* says, "The hero most often views his flaw as a defense mechanism he needs for his survival. The hero does not view his flaw as a flaw, but as a way of coping with life, as a behavior that protects his life metaphorically or perhaps even physically. That is why the hero has not already let go of his flaw—he actually does believe that he needs it." (19)

Lucy's mother died when she was a girl, and since the passing of her father a year before the story starts, she's been totally alone in the world. Fantasizing about ideal happily-ever-afters and faraway lands makes her life bearable without risking more pain and loss.

The protagonist's belief that his flaw protects him isn't totally false or without merit. It truly does protect him from some emotional or physical pain. But more significantly it blocks him from attaining something important in life, something so precious it would ultimately be worth any potential pain. So while the flaw safeguards the protagonist from a specific negative condition, it also imprisons him from an equally specific positive condition. In *While You Were Sleeping*, Lucy's flaw protects her from excruciating loneliness. It's also preventing her from having a real relationship with someone she can laugh and grow old with.

Flaws create conflict every which way the protagonist turns. He tries to pursue his external goal, but a flawed decision trips him up. He tries to gain the support of an ally, but his flawed behavior sabotages the very relationship vital to his success. He tries to figure out what's the right thing to do in a difficult situation, but his flaw clouds his values and judgment with doubts and questions.

Flaws that hinder and hurt the protagonist alone are fine in average stories, but better stories kick it up another notch. The best stories use the protagonist's flaw to deepen and broaden the stakes. So long as his flaw trips up only the protagonist, the stakes associated with his character arc are limited. In addition to hurting himself, the flaw needs a moral component that impacts other characters.

Angela Ackerman and Becca Puglisi in *The Negative Trait Thesaurus* defines *flaws* as "traits that damage or minimize relationships and do not take into account the well-being of others. They also tend to be self-focused rather than other-focused." (14) This dual psychological-moral nature of a flaw is so essential that John Truby says in *The Anatomy of Story*, "The hero must overcome a moral flaw and learn how to act properly toward other people. A character with a moral need is always hurting others in some way (his moral weakness) at the beginning of the story." (41)

When a flaw hurts other people it layers a psychological trait with additional complexity. A psychological flaw which handicaps only the protagonist from fully experiencing life makes for a rather flat character arc. But when that psychological flaw is amplified by a moral weakness, the stakes concerning the character arc expand into the community of the entire story. A dual psychological-moral flaw provides the protagonist with not only an inner obstacle to overcome, but a destination—a lesson to be learned.

In *While You Were Sleeping*, Lucy's flaw holds her back from accomplishing her dreams, but it also threatens the health and happiness of the Callaghan family.

In *Casablanca* (1942), Rick's flaw of cynicism keeps him trapped in the past, but it also hurts the woman he loves and even threatens the entire European underground resistance effort against the Nazis.

In *Frozen* (2013), Elsa's flaw of emotional repression stifles her creative gifts and isolates her from her family, but it also hurts her sister and eventually plunges the entire kingdom into perpetual winter. Not to mention ruining Kristoff's ice business.

To find a character's flaw or weakness, look at what they're afraid of or the lies they believe about themselves. Usually both fears and lies can be traced to an emotionally wounding event in the character's backstory. Often this event is reinforced in their subconscious by their upbringing or lesser substantiating events.

Depending on their personality, a character can believe one of nine basic lies about themselves. Each of these lies generates a specific fear that shapes and informs their habits and behaviors. The following list of nine lies, fears, and their corresponding negative behaviors is adapted from Don Richard Riso and Russ Hudson's *The Wisdom of the Enneagram: The Complete Guide to Psychological and Spiritual Growth for the Nine Personality Types*, Wendy Appel's *InsideOut Enneagram*, and Lynette Sheppard's *The Everyday Enneagram.*

TYPE ONE

Basic Lie: "It's not okay to make mistakes. Life is about correcting errors."

Basic Fear: Being bad or defective.

Behavior: Angry, resentful, critical perfectionist.

TYPE TWO

Basic Lie: "It's not okay to have your own needs. I give others what they need."

Basic Fear: Being unworthy of love.

Behavior: Proud, manipulative, needs to be needed.

TYPE THREE

Basic Lie: "It's not okay to have your own feelings and identity. Life is about looking successful."

Basic Fear: Being worthless.

Behavior: Deceitful, vain, chasing after success.

TYPE FOUR

Basic Lie: "It's not okay to be too functional or too happy. I'm different. Something essential is missing from my life."

Basic Fear: Being insignificant.

Behavior: Self-indulgent, envious, ashamed.

TYPE FIVE

Basic Lie: "It's not okay to be comfortable in the world. Knowledge will keep me safe, but emotions are dangerous."

Basic Fear: Being incapable or incompetent.

Behavior: Stingy, avaricious, useless specialization.

TYPE SIX

Basic Lie: "It's not okay to trust yourself. Stay vigilant, because the world's a dangerous place."

Basic Fear: Being without support.

Behavior: Worrier, insecure, tests loyalties.

TYPE SEVEN

Basic Lie: "It's not okay to depend on anyone for anything. Life is about experiencing as much as possible."

Basic Fear: Being deprived or trapped in pain.

Behavior: Indulgent, irresponsible, escapist.

TYPE EIGHT

Basic Lie: "It's not okay to be vulnerable or to trust anyone. Only the strong survive."

Basic Fear: Being harmed or controlled by others.

Behavior: Lustful, vengeful, dominating.

TYPE NINE

Basic Lie: "It's not okay to assert yourself. Life is about harmony and going with the flow."

Basic Fear: Losing connection with others.

Behavior: Complacent, indifferent, stubbornly neglectful.

In *While You Were Sleeping*, Lucy's wounding backstory event is the death of her parents, specifically and most recently her beloved father. She believes the lie that something—specifically an idealized Dream Prince—will fill the painful void left by her father's passing. This causes her to give in to self-indulgent fantasies about marrying the handsome stranger who passes her by every day on his way to work.

Of course, the opening problem can't be all bad news or else the protagonist would run for the hills. He'd never make the necessary trek through the Great Swampy Middle where real internal change occurs. What makes him stick around until eventually committing to the story?

The opening problem, even if it's gift-wrapped as a golden opportunity, spells trouble for the protagonist with a capital T. Nevertheless, even while it challenges the protagonist's flaw head-on, there's an integral component of it that promises to satisfy the protagonist's deepest desire. It's the hook in the protagonist's jaw that yanks him into the story.

Look again at the nine Basic Fears listed above. Flip them on their heads, and they point to the character's deepest desires. For example, if Lucy is afraid of feeling unseen and insignificant, then her deepest desire is to feel valued and seen as important to someone. She will do *anything* to achieve that internal goal.

The Callaghan family overwhelms Lucy with love and approval. They see her as the brave woman who saved their son's life, and as their son's presumed fiancee, she's automatically an important member of the family. Despite her best efforts to escape the situation, there's no way she's emotionally strong enough to walk away from the chance to fulfill her strongest desire.

Of course, the protagonist's deepest desire isn't necessarily what he really *needs*. More than likely, so long as he's denying personal responsibility for his problems, his deepest desire erroneously centers and is dependent in some fundamental way on others. He's not trying to fulfill his own desire. He's busy trying to get someone else to do it for him. Which pretty much guarantees the problem is only going to get worse until he learns what he needs to achieve self-empowerment over his situation.

Lucy *desires* for a Dream Prince to rescue her from loneliness. She *needs* to learn it's up to her to pursue her dreams and live a full life, which at the end of the movie she's quitting her job to do. That she also gets an improved version of her desire—the hero showing up with an engagement ring and marriage proposal—is an unexpected bonus for having learned the lesson.

To figure out what lesson the character needs to learn, look at the Basic Lie and flip it on its head. For example, Lucy is a Type Four. She starts out believing the lie that something essential to her happiness is missing from her life. By the end of the movie, she learns she's already got everything she needs to pursue her dreams and try to make them come true.

The lesson of every story involves redeeming the best part of the character—their strength. It's about achieving a healthy psychological balance, not changing their personality or making them do something unrecognizable. Flaws are simply strengths that have been corrupted by fear until they deteriorated into self-defeating and hurtful behaviors. The lesson learned near the end of the story represents the character's inherent potential finally realized.

As much as the flaw has hurt the protagonist and others, some people don't want him to overcome it. There are some who actually rely and depend upon the protagonist's behaving badly. These characters belong to his old support system. Addiction therapy refers to these kind of people as "enablers." They make it easier for him to not have to change, because well-intentioned or not, they never challenge him to be a better human being. They don't rock the boat. While enablers may be lovers, friends, family, etc., they can also be circumstances. For example, in *Good Will Hunting* (1998) the character uses his janitorial job to hide from his own potential as a mathematical genius.

As the protagonist gradually transforms during his journey through the Great Swampy Middle, enabling characters in supporting roles experience their own tests and trials. The protagonist's gradual growth away from his flaw destabilizes their status quo. If they resist this change, their roles in the story may shift from allies to opposition. If they are brave enough to accept the change rippling through their own lives, they earn a share in the protagonist's victory at the end.

FURTHER READING

Suggestions to deepen your understanding of character flaws:

Angela Ackerman & Becca Puglisi's *The Negative Trait Thesaurus: A Writer's Guide to Character Flaws.* Available in ebook and print on Amazon and wherever books are sold.

Don Richard Riso and Russ Hudson's *The Wisdom of the Enneagram: The Complete Guide to Psychological and Spiritual Growth for the Nine Personality Types.* Available in print on Amazon and wherever books are sold.

Wendy Appel's *InsideOut Enneagram: The Game-Changing Guide for Leaders.* Available in print on Amazon and wherever books are sold.

Lynette Sheppard's *The Everyday Enneagram: A Personality Map for Enhancing Your Work, Love, and Life... Every Day.* Available in ebook and print on Amazon and wherever books are sold.

Beatrice Chestnut's *The Complete Enneagram: 27 Paths to Greater Self-Knowledge.* Available in ebook and print on Amazon and wherever books are sold.

Structure

Okay, so you're suited up, ready to dash through the fictional equivalent of the Everglades toward that beacon of hope called the Midpoint. It should be easy to find, since it's suppose to be really big and it's smack in the middle of... um, somewhere.

Time to break out the well-prepared adventurer's best friend—a map of the terrain. This is not the kind of map that dictates what happens when, like a GPS ordering you, "Turn left at alligator crossing, proceed north to bleached human skull."

Instead, story structure is like a map that tracks the highs and lows of various threads running through the story. It's totally up to the individual writer how to interpret those highs and lows according to his own unique artistic vision.

Why is a basic understanding of story structure necessary to mastering the Midpoint? Like any geometric shape, the middle is always defined by the area surrounding it. The depth of change wrought by the Midpoint can only be properly comprehended through an awareness of how it divides the story in two and throws those halves into stark contrast.

Some people get a little nervous at the mention of structure. It sounds a lot like "stricture," as in restricting creativity and inspiration.

They may confuse structuring a story with structuring how they write the story, and fear their imagination being buried in an avalanche of outlines, graphs, and charts. (While there is a diagram near the back of this book, it serves as a visual aide, not a GPS coordinate.)

Story structure emotionally connects the audience with the story by weaving together plot, conflict, and character into a meaningful unity of purpose. It's a support system for the writer's unique vision, guaranteeing that all the story parts are functioning to their maximum potential. A reader unconsciously senses when everything is working together. That's the moment he relaxes into the story, gives over his trust to the author, and blissfully loses track of time.

Story structure is universal to not only all genres and types of stories, but it's also universal to human experience. It resonates with each person everywhere, no matter their life circumstances. Different cultures may emphasize certain themes over others, but humans are essentially the same the world over. Charles Dickens summed up the secret of his world-renowned success as the ability to "Make them laugh, make them cry, make them wait." That's exactly what story structure is about.

Most writers have encountered the Three-Act Structure concept. In brief, Act One (first 25%) introduces the reader to a protagonist who urgently wants something specific. Act Two (middle 50%) details the escalating trouble he goes through trying to get it. Act Three (final 25%) shows the physical and emotional consequences of his attempt.

The Midpoint falls right in the middle of that *escalating trouble* part where the protagonist is trying his hardest to reach his goal. Imagine that three-act design cut in two. First half: a protagonist's urgent want for something specific leads to escalating trouble. Second half: trying to get what he urgently wants results in physical and emotional consequences.

Lots of room for creative interpretation there, but a little bit more detail wouldn't hurt and might even make the adventure a bit more interesting. Like, is that boulder up ahead something the hero should skirt around or climb up on top of to get a better view?

That's where sequences come in. Dan Decker in *Anatomy of a Screenplay* calls sequences "the blood pressure of your [story]." (185) A sequence is a series of scenes with its own mini-Three-Act-Structure. Each sequence has its own supporting goal, conflict, and motivation advancing the larger story's goal, conflict, and motivation. The early scenes in a sequence establish the lead character's want and why it's important to the larger story. The middle scenes follow the increasing difficulty he has in getting it. The final scenes show whether he gets it or not, and the consequences to his larger story goal.

Pilar Alessandra in *The Coffee Break Screenwriter* says in order to identify sequences, look for those places in the story where there's a major twist, or the stakes rise, or the character's forced to make a big, emotional choice. It's easier to tap into the rhythm of the story if the writer doesn't think about the story as separate scenes, but rather as clusters of scenes. (28-29)

For example, suppose the protagonist in a romantic suspense has a story goal of recovering stolen top secret files before they are sold to the highest bidder? An early sequence's supporting goal might be to shadow the prime suspect until he can find out where the files are hidden. That activity and the associated complications link together a group of scenes that all, in one way or another, are concerned with *shadowing the suspect.*

Then something twisty happens. The suspect gets in trouble. She's stranded, and the protagonist is suddenly confronted with a new choice. He risks breaking his cover to play Good Samaritan and earn her trust. That's the next group of scenes, all about *earning her trust.*

Sequences are tied together by events, which are special, high-octane scenes where something big happens in the external plot that compels the character to make a decision or choice that has clear consequences and reveals the internal thoughts and motivations of the character. Linda J. Cowgill in *The Art of Plotting* says, "Decisions and choices can come anywhere in a [story's] plot. But major decisions and choices are most effective when played at the [story's] structural turning points." (84)

This is one of the chief ways plot and character are woven together in a balanced and satisfying whole. The external plot applies pressure on the character to change direction and turn either toward deeper vice or higher virtue. Cowgill explains that forcing characters to make difficult decisions and choices is the principal way to "show, don't tell" who they are. Instead of paper dolls, taped together from backstory and attitudes, they become three-dimensional people whose actions shape their destiny and drive the story. (85)

If you've already figured out that the definition for *events* sounds very similar in function to the Midpoint, reward yourself with a handful of trail mix and enjoy the clean, soapy scent of swamp orchids for a moment. Because the Midpoint is one of the biggest events in the whole story.

Eight sequences divide the Three-Act Structure in a 2-4-2 breakdown: two sequences in the first act, four in the second act, and two in the third act. Each sequence explores a different aspect of character, conflict, and theme, building the universal dynamics of dramatic change into the story. Each sequence ends or begins with a big, bold, definite turning point event tightly knotting the internal and external conflicts together.

ACT 1

Sequence 1 (0% - 12.5%) — Establishes the tone and kind of story it is (sentimental, snarky, light, dark, etc.). Something essential to the protagonist's physical and/or emotional wellbeing is crumbling away, gradually disintegrating the world that's familiar to him. Main characters are introduced striving to accomplish something important to them. Strengths, flaws, and motivations are hinted at. ***Ending turning point event: Problem*** (10% - 12.5) — Change presents the protagonist with a problem. The antagonist instigates either bad news or a golden opportunity that challenges the protagonist's flaw, forcing him to make a decision.

Sequence 2 (12.5% - 25%) — Early encounters with obstacles establishes the physical and emotional stakes. The pros and cons of the thematic premise are debated. If the protagonist is eager to accept the challenge of the Problem event, other characters relying on maintaining the status quo try to talk him out of it. If the protagonist is hesitant to rock the boat himself, a mentor shows up to provide a helpful push. ***Ending turning point event: Commitment*** (22.5% - 25%) — Protagonist proactively commits to a plan that will thrust him into a distinctly new set of circumstances, while resisting genuine change (often personified in some way by the antagonist).

ACT 2

Sequence 3 (25% - 37.5%) — The protagonist is locked in to the world of the story as he takes the road of least resistance, eliminating the easiest and most obvious options first. As he gathers the tools or allies he needs from new or existing supporting characters, he also runs into some new enemies. Nevertheless, his plan seems to be working. ***Ending turning point event: Fear Made Real*** (35% - 37.5) — The antagonist punches back, delivering a surprising loss to the protagonist that makes things personal. Glimpsing his worst fear, the protagonist briefly falters.

Sequence 4 (37.5% - 50%)— The protagonist plans to take the fight to the antagonist. Believing he knows everything he needs to achieve his goal, he digs deep down and closes in for the confrontation. However, important alliances may strain and crack apart under the pressure. ***Ending turning point event: Midpoint, part 1*** (47.5% - 50%) — The protagonist glimpses a possible outcome to the story as he is cut off at the pass, trapped, or attacked by the antagonist who is onto him and his plan. Turns out the protagonist didn't know enough after all about his own flaws or his opponent's strengths, and the lesson delivers a powerful wakeup call.

Sequence 5 — *Beginning turning point event: Midpoint, part 2* (50% - 52.5%) — The protagonist recognizes his flaw is the major obstacle to his own external goal. Major character roles reverse as loyalties shift. Questions and answers generate a new way of pursuing the external goal. **Sequence** (50% - 62.5%): The protagonist's efforts to pursue his goal in the first half of the story have dug a deep hole he attempts to climb out of in the second half of the story. But it isn't going to be easy. The antagonist strips away the protagonist's physical, emotional, and/or spiritual support system. Rules, beliefs, even relationships that the protagonist once relied on for security won't work anymore as they disintegrate in front of his eyes.

Sequence 6 — *Beginning turning point event: Hope Lost* (62.5% - 65%) — The antagonist delivers the knock-out punch to the protagonist, breaking his will to continue. All hope seems lost. The mentor who encouraged and helped prepare him for this mission may even die. Or, it's a moment of premature success and celebration, but hard-earned wisdom warns the protagonist even this silver cloud has a dark lining. **Sequence** (62.5% - 75%): Hopeless, forsaken, the protagonist temporarily gives up on his goal as a lost cause and seeks to crawl into a hole somewhere. There's no mentor around this time to give him a helpful shove. Or, he lulls himself into a false sense of security, mistaking living like a fugitive under the antagonist's radar for "good enough."

ACT 3

Sequence 7 – *Beginning turning point event: New Direction* (75% - 77.5%) — The antagonist jeopardizes a relationship of vital importance to the protagonist, forcing him to adopt a new plan and nobler goal. **Sequence** (75% - 87.5%): The protagonist rallies allies and gathers equipment to urgently execute his new plan, and sets out to deliberately do what he's been desperately avoiding all along: confront his worst fear. For a brief period of time, his crazy plan seems to work, too.

Sequence 8 – *Beginning turning point event: Sacrifice* (87.5% - 90%) — The protagonist either sacrifices any chance of personal gain for the sake of others, or confronts the antagonist and suffers a bitter, gut-wrenching defeat. **Sequence** (87.5% - 100%): The protagonist digs down deep one final time and executes a new plan stripped of all selfish concerns. If he sacrificed something precious at the beginning turning point event, then what's left is the public confrontation with the antagonist, where he fails big time. Or, if he already confronted the antagonist at the beginning turning point event, then what's left is the (often public) sacrifice of the last thing holding him back from genuine internal growth. In completing his internal arc, the path is cleared to receive unexpected grace, redemption, and/or reward.

See, the protagonist has his own Great Swampy Middle to hack through, too. When he reaches the Midpoint, instead of the story being over like he probably hoped, he discovers he's got to hack his way right back out again. The key is that the last four sequences are basically a repeat of the first four, with ramped-up intensity, heightened stakes, and a new awareness on the part of the protagonist. That new awareness of his own flaws and strengths, ambitions and opposition, relationships and loyalties, is what makes the protagonist essentially have to repeat the story over again. Except now he's got more at risk than ever before and he's in the middle of Act Two, deep behind enemy lines in the antagonist's dramatic territory.

— *Sequence 1* and *Sequence 5* are both about unsettling and stripping away the protagonist's support system. In Sequence 1, little earthquake swarms disrupt longterm behavior patterns and external support systems, making his comfort zone increasingly unsustainable. In Sequence 5, the antagonist sets off a big earthquake right under the protagonist's belief systems and relationships, leaving him with nowhere to go.

— *Sequence 2* and *Sequence 6* are both concerned with weighing the costs of going forward and whether or not the physical/emotional stakes are worth it. A reluctant protagonist wonders what to do next. A willing protagonist thinks he knows, but doesn't. In Sequence 2, other characters provide assistance, both for and against, in making his difficult moral choice. In Sequence 6, he's physically or emotionally isolated from assistance and has to make an even tougher moral choice all on his own.

— *Sequence 3* and *Sequence 7* are both about gathering allies to execute a new plan. In Sequence 3, that plan is about taking the easy way. Sometimes the easiest way is attempting to avoid the antagonist altogether. In Sequence 7, the plan is not only hard, it's probably crazy, because it's deliberately designed to provoke the protagonist's worst fear into manifestation.

— *Sequence 4* and *Sequence 8* are both about taking the fight to the antagonist, even when allies fall by the wayside, leaving the protagonist the last one standing. In Sequence 4, his plan is based on overconfident assumptions about his own strength and the antagonist's flaws. In Sequence 8, the experiential knowledge of his own flaws and the antagonist's strengths informs his efforts.

Here's an example of Hesba Stretton's 1.5 million-plus bestseller *Jessica's First Prayer* broken down into parallel sequences demonstrating the repeated sequence structure. It's a 10,000 word novella about a neglected urchin girl (an adorable antagonist) who befriends a greedy coffee peddler (the protagonist) living a secret double life as a respected church-keeper.

Sequence 1 and Sequence 5 are both about loosening miserly Daniel's grip on his double-life and greedy motives. In Sequence 1, starving little street urchin Jessica disrupts Daniel's day-to-day business-as-usual at his coffee-stall, and he tries to drive her away, but eventually gives her some crusts for breakfast. How are the stakes expanded and amplified in Sequence 5? His whole business is on the line and he intends to set the police on her to keep her away. But she pierces his miserly motives with a simple prayer that God repay him for her free breakfasts. Only Daniel knows he's never given anything to anyone except Jessica, and then only dregs and crusts. He fears God's reckoning day.

Sequence 2 and Sequence 6 are both about Daniel's debating the professional, social, and spiritual risks of loving money. In Sequence 2, Jessica's tempted to steal a penny but gives it up, which Daniel knows is more than he could have done. He agrees to let her come back for breakfast once a week. How are the stakes expanded and amplified in Sequence 6? The minister entrusts her with an entire shilling every week to pay for daily breakfasts. Daniel worries it could mean exposure and closing down his coffee-stall business, but he can't give up that much extra money every week.

Sequence 3 and Sequence 7 are both about Daniel's gathering allies to implement a new plan. In Sequence 3, Jessica follows Daniel to church and uncovers his double-life as a respected church-keeper. Terrified his secret will be exposed, he takes the easiest way out and enlists the police to keep her away from church, but she slips back. How are the stakes expanded and amplified in Sequence 7? Jessica quits showing up for breakfast or church. Worried crazy about the child, Daniel risks exposure by enlisting the minister's help to search for her. Finding her deathly ill, he repents for loving dirty money better than a poor, helpless, friendless child.

Sequence 4 and Sequence 8 are both about Daniel's confrontation with Jessica over exposing his secret double-life to the great people of the church. In Sequence 4, the minister's children discover Jessica hiding in church and Daniel nearly faints with anxiety when he's ordered to seat her in front of the pews by the pulpit steps. How are the stakes expanded and amplified in Sequence 8? Daniel abandons his business to dedicate himself to nursing Jessica in his own home. He summons the minister to Jessica's deathbed, and confesses his secret double-life. He'd give every penny he has for the child's life. Jessica prays and is restored to health.

This is the pattern of human change and development in real life as well as fiction. 1. The status quo becomes unsustainable. 2. Figure out your options and count the costs. 3. Take the easiest way to minimize necessary change. 4. Learn how much you didn't know, and pick up the pieces from your mistakes. Rinse and repeat until lasting growth is achieved. The cycle is usually uncomfortable enough, however, that people don't relish going through it again and require the motivation of a powerful wakeup call.

What event is powerful enough to trigger such a major awakening and reversal? The Midpoint. Late writing guru Blake Snyder in *Save the Cat Strikes Back!* calls it "the Grand Central Station of plot points, the nerve center." (51) It's created from two major events generating a cause-and-effect reversal of the story's direction. The first half of the Midpoint is the ending turning point event of Sequence 4. The second half of the Midpoint is the beginning turning point event of Sequence 5. These two events tie the two halves of the story together like twin scarlet cords tied into a bow.

The most dramatically effective locations for these two events occur at 47.5% - 50% for the first event, and 50% - 52.5% for the second event. The precise percentages directly relate to the power of focused intensity. The protagonist needs a sharp jolt to wake him up to the necessity to change his ways. A sprawling, meandering Midpoint might disturb his psychological slumber, but will fail to sufficiently roust him from his familiar bed of false beliefs.

Likewise, if the Midpoint events occur too soon or too late, it will throw the whole story off-balance with shrunken, underdeveloped sequences on one side and bloated, overextended sequences on the other. Most readers won't consciously know or care if the Midpoint lands a few pages off-center one way or the other. But they will *feel* it on an instinctive subconscious level that impacts their reading pleasure and satisfaction.

What about those other percentages associated with sequences and beginning or ending events? To the writer, they are landmarks helping him recognize where he's at in the story and where he's going when he gets there. To the characters, they are urgent developments that keep him engaged with the story when the going gets hard.

The truth is, characters don't really want to change, even if they start the story wishing for a different life or improved circumstances.

Change on the inside where it really makes a difference requires hard work and commitment. The protagonist is quite liable to find a relatively easy spot in the Everglades and want to stay there for the rest of the story. Sure, the mosquitoes drive him crazy, but he hasn't seen an alligator in a while and he can call Animal Control to relocate the occasional stray rattlesnake. It takes the percentage marks to announce, "Time's up! Back on your feet!" and get him moving again down increasingly challenging paths until he reaches The End.

Dan Decker in *Anatomy of a Screenplay* says not to stress over forcing specific events to happen by certain page numbers. If the story is well-crafted, everything will fall naturally into place. "Page count is a by-product of proper structure, not the goal of proper structure." (98) While it's unlikely every novel or movie or television show will hit all the marks exactly, odds are the closer they come the stronger the story will be.

FURTHER READING

Suggestions to deepen your understanding of story structure:

Blake Snyder's *Save the Cat!* books. Each one adds and expands so well upon the others, that I think of the trilogy as a set. Available in Kindle edition on Amazon and in print wherever books are sold.

David Howard's *How to Build a Great Screenplay: A Master Class in Storytelling for Film.* Available in ebook and print on Amazon and wherever books are sold.

Robert McKee's *Story: Substance, Structure, Style, and the Principles of Screenwriting.* Chapter 6, "Structure and Meaning." Available in ebook and print on Amazon and wherever books are sold.

My book, *Story Bones: How to X-Ray Any Novel for Plot, Conflict, and Character.* Currently about $3 for the Kindle edition and less than $10 for the print edition. Buy the paperback on Amazon, and get the ebook for more than 50% off.

Creating Tension

Armed with your trusty map, you now know precisely the Midpoint's location relative to other important landmarks on the story landscape. Examining the scarlet cord in your hand marking the trail through the Great Swampy Middle to the Midpoint and beyond, you discover something. It isn't ordinary string or rope or twine. It's a fuse!

Yes, the fuse is lit, and there are three specific places in the story where something is going to go *boom!* (If you guessed the Midpoint is one of those three, go roast some s'mores over the fire, because you're right.) *Boom!* doesn't necessarily mean anything has to literally explode, but something does happen that shakes the protagonist's world to its foundations. In a romance, it could be as simple as a kiss. In a mystery, chances are it's a body drop. In a western, it might be a literal brushfire.

Stories in any genre rely upon one essential ingredient above all others to keep readers turning the pages. It's experienced as the driving question, "What happens next?" It's the essence of unpredictability, and it's created by building **tension**. The carefully crafted balancing act between what the reader *fears* will happen versus what she *hopes* will happen keeps the flame of anticipation burning. David Howard in *How* *to Build a Great Screenplay* says, "A story needs highs and lows; the audience's hopes must be encouraged, and also its fears." (337)

What are these highs and lows, and where are the most dramatically effective locations for them to occur in a story?

Well, before answering those questions, let's explore how tension works. Tension belongs on every page, but not every page is going to go *boom!* It's a matter of degrees. Small tensions are like little firecrackers. *Snap! Crack! Pop!* Big tensions are like bursting rockets. *Whoosh! Pow!* The biggest tensions of all are like bombs going off in the middle of a swamp, shaking the ground and hurling giant boulders through the air. *Ka-BOOM!*

Those small tensions, the little firecrackers that kindle the big fires, are lit in scenes. Every scene, in order to advance the story, ends with a change of some kind in the character's emotional and/or physical circumstances. Closer to his desired outcome, or further away from it than before. Full of hope, or overwhelmed by fear. A high or a low.

Of course, sometimes the reader understands better than the character what to hope for or what to fear. Informed by superior knowledge, experience, or sophistication, the reader may fear the character will attain a misguided goal or hope he fails to achieve it (or at least wise up before it's too late). In cases like this, a high for the character is a low for the reader and vice versa.

As in an early scene from Nora Roberts' romantic suspense *The Witness.* A rebellious sixteen year-old girl goes on a forbidden shopping spree in the mall and connects with a girl from school. To the attention-starved teenager the scene ends on a high, as she believes she's made a friend. But the reader worries the untrustworthy acquaintance will take dangerous advantage of the inexperienced girl. To the reader, the scene ends on a fear-fueled low.

Jiang Hongyan / Shutterstock

These small sparks of tension are vital building blocks to a successful story, but by themselves are insufficient to elevate it above a static modulation. The big bursting rocket tensions occur at the beginning or end of sequences. Remember, sequences are a series of scenes unified by a common goal, conflict, and motivation. Some sequences end "down," with the character's apparent failure, while other sequences end "up," with the character's success.

As in the third sequence of Suzanne Collins' dystopian bestseller *The Hunger Games.* The majority of the scenes focus on Katniss' and Peeta's training and preparation for the Games. The sequence culminates with their televised interviews. Katniss barely squeaks by, but Peeta is a mesmerizing success when he confesses to an unrequited love for his partner from District Twelve. Even while it throws Katniss for a dizzying emotional loop, the event ends the sequence on a high regarding their goal of winning support for their survival.

To balance and contrast the greatest moment of tension in the whole story—the climax near the end—there needs to be even greater moments than those offered by sequences alone. That's where the biggest bomb events come in. The highs and lows significant enough to amp up the reader's anticipation of the end occur at three key turning point events in the story. These turning points are:

The **Commitment** event, where the protagonist is locked into the story and is compelled to come up with a plan to solve the problem introduced in Act One.

The **Midpoint** event(s), where the protagonist sees his flaw for what it is and his loyalties shift, causing him to change his goal or his way of pursuing it.

The **New Direction** event, where a threat to an important relationship forces the protagonist to adopt a new plan and nobler goal.

Boom!... BOOM!... Boom!

Paul Joseph Gulino in *Screenwriting: the Sequence Approach* says the bottom of Act Two doesn't necessarily have to always be a low point. (17) While it often is expressed as a "dark night of the soul," its dramatic purpose allows it to also be expressed at certain times as a "false victory." Blake Snyder in *Save the Cat!* defines the changeable nature of this event by its unique relationship with the Midpoint: "These two points are a matched set. It's because the two beats are the inverse of each other." (84) The general rule of thumb is that if the Midpoint is "up," then the other is "down." If the Midpoint is "down," then the other is "up." Even if both events *seem* headed in the same direction, something significant about them must be fundamentally opposite.

(Snyder identifies the Midpoint's opposite event as the "All Is Lost" moment followed by a "Dark Night of the Soul" stage comprising the last 9% of Act Two, and distinguishes it from the New Direction event that breaks into Act Three. While I agree with much of his characterization of the final sequence in Act Two, I believe the dramatic intensity of the Midpoint's opposite event is more closely associated with the hinge point linking the Acts.)

Any of these three key turning point events can be highs or lows. All of them need not be the same, however. Mix them up. Make two of them highs and one low, or two lows and one high. Each of them provides escalating previews of either a positive or negative possible outcome. By the time Act Three arrives, the reader has experienced wildly opposite extremes of hope and fear. What matters is that the reader heads toward the ending feeling anything is possible. Howard says, "One or the other must be the opposite [of the climax] or else you will go into the third act with your resolution being predictable." (338)

Of course, the Midpoint accomplishes much more than setting off explosive tension as a major high or low point in the Great Swampy Middle. Blake Snyder in *Save the Cat!* likens deciding what kind of Midpoint your story requires to nailing a spike into a wall. The whole story hangs upon it. (84) Though every writer approaches their story differently, determining the Midpoint first is an amazingly helpful guide to crafting the other major turning points.

For example, perhaps a writer decides the Midpoint will be a high-stakes "low" for the protagonist in the story, where he seems further away than ever from his goal even as he takes a big step in his internal growth. The writer can follow the scarlet cord of the Midpoint directly to the break into Act Three and craft an opposite event. Perhaps a "high" where the protagonist gets his goal, only to discover it comes with a huge and unexpected "but" attached. Unwinding the red cord in the other direction, the writer can setup Act One to culminate in a "low" testing the protagonist's commitment to his purpose.

J.R.R. Tolkien's classic fantasy *The Hobbit* is an enduring example of two lows and a high. At the Commitment event, Bilbo Baggins finds himself lost and abandoned by his companions in the goblins' tunnels. He determines to press ahead on his own, but first he has to pass the murderous creature Gollum's riddle test. As the culmination of the story's second sequence, this event locks Bilbo into the story. From this moment on, he "owns" his decision to go on the quest after Smaug's treasure. But it also gives both Bilbo and the reader a preview of a possible negative outcome to the adventure. At this point it's entirely plausible that at the end inexperienced Bilbo could get separated from his companions and die alone at the hands of a fiendish monster. Definitely a low moment, where success seems far away and fear runs strong.

Then at the Midpoint, Bilbo finds himself lost again. This time he's with his companions, wandering in the poisonous maze of Mirkwood forest. Driven by starvation, they leave the path in search of food and become separated from one another. Bilbo's subsequent rescue of his companions from giant spiders makes a different person of him, "much fiercer and bolder in spite of an empty stomach." Even though Bilbo saves his friends from immediate death, they still seem impossibly far from their story goal. This is another low moment, a glimpse of a potential negative outcome. They could all die on this quest.

At the New Direction event, Bilbo saves his companions from a dragon attack and leads them courageously into the heart of Smaug's mountain. Once again the little hobbit braves underground tunnels and a bloodthirsty creature. But this time "he was a very different hobbit from the one that had run out without a pocket-hankerchief from Bag-End long ago" in Act One. He's brave, and he's not alone. He's their leader, with ideas and plans of his own. This event, though fraught with danger, previews for the reader a positive possible outcome. One where Bilbo and his friends find the treasure they've sought so long and hard for, and Bilbo becomes "a burglar indeed" when he claims a fabulous diamond for his own.

Sometimes hanging onto a positive ending provides more than enough conflict to occupy Act Three. Bilbo's and his friends' story resolves on a satisfying high, but it's tinged with some bittersweetness. Not all of Bilbo's companions survive their own flaws, and some of the treasure must be sacrificed to prevent senseless bloodshed. But Bilbo accomplishes the essence of what he set out to do. He went on an adventure and succeeded at recovering the dragon's treasure.

Suppose a writer decides he wants the Midpoint to represent a "high" and give the protagonist a motivating preview of a happily-ever-after ending? Tracing the scarlet cord backwards to the break into Act Two, he might decide to zigzag the tension with a "low" where the protagonist stoutly rejects the very person or mission that will bring him fulfillment. The Midpoint's opposite event at the break into Act Three snaps easily into place as a "low" where the protagonist instinctively and unreservedly embraces the person/cause but is physically far removed from attaining what he wants.

As in James Oliver Curwood's bestselling historical romance *The Alaskan*. Alaskan pioneer Alan Holt's cynical stoicism is jolted when mysterious passenger Mary Standish elects him as her escort aboard the *Nome*. She gets under his skin, despite contradictory evidence of a possible connection between Mary and his sworn enemy. At the Commitment event, Mary stuns Alan by appealing for his help staging her own death. Deciding she's either a fool or a liar, he roughly rejects her. She tells him she must really die then, since she cannot reach their destination alive. This is a low point in both the plot and the romance. It previews a possible outcome where not only the hero and heroine aren't happily together ever after, but one of them just might be dead!

Alan comes to bitterly regret not coming to Mary's aid when she needed him. Believing her lost at sea, he lives with her ghost haunting his grieving, lovesick heart. Then at the Midpoint, he finds her not only alive and well, but calmly awaiting him at his remote ranch. More a woman of mystery than ever, Mary offers few answers to increasingly disturbing questions even while she earns the unreserved devotion of Alan's friends and household. Alan watches the woman of his dreams fit as naturally and vitally into his life as breathing. This is a high point, providing both the hero and reader with a powerful glimpse of a possible happily ever after for the couple.

There is no secret that will not eventually be revealed. Mary's are no exception. She's the runaway bride of Alan's hated enemy, a man of unlimited power and evil. Their love forbidden, Alan protects her honor by removing himself to ride the range. At the New Direction event, a messenger delivers a life-and-death summons from Mary. Their mutual enemy has caught up with her, and she's trapped at the ranch. Without pause, Alan races to her aid. This event redeems Alan's earlier abandonment of her cause at the break into Act Two, but nevertheless is a low point in the story. The heroine's jeopardy puts the happily ever after ending inherent in romances at dire risk of failure and echoes the taste of death suggested earlier by the Commitment event.

Of course, it wouldn't qualify as a romance if it didn't ultimately achieve its promised happily ever after for the hero and heroine. But Alan and Mary pass through a literal hail of bullets and baptism of fire in Act Three before earning their satisfying ending.

What if the protagonist is in such a deep rut he digs in his heels at every opportunity to change and the writer has to drag him kicking and screaming along every inch of the character arc? Perhaps the writer determines to make the Midpoint a "low," where the protagonist confronts his flaw but freaks out in despair. The crimson cord of the Midpoint may guide the writer to a "low" event breaking into Act Two. Maybe the protagonist is about to quit the story before it really gets under way, believing his flaw is justified, but finally commits when he realizes this may be a special exception to the rule he's been living by. The protagonist has been so stiff-necked through the story, he needs one more "low" to test him at the break into Act Three and to counterbalance the reader's expectation of a happy ending. Because this is the Midpoint's opposite, the writer gives the scarlet cord a twist: the antagonist packs up his marbles and tries to quit the story, leaving the protagonist in a painful lurch.

As in Debbie Macomber's contemporary romance *The Way to a Man's Heart*. When stodgy literary professor Grey meets merry waitress Meghan, his life takes on an expected sparkle. After their first kiss, at the Commitment event Meghan prepares for their first date, wanting everything perfect. The untimely and messy death of the dishwater submarines that hope. Then Grey shows up right on time, and mistakes her reluctance to open the door on her domestic disaster as proof she's got another man in her apartment. What's at stake is the romance breaking up before it's even well under way. These two are obviously meant for each other, but their insecurities could prevent them from ever finding that out.

Overcoming their rocky start, the couple begins dating. Grey finds warmth and acceptance among her large, loving family, and Meghan gains confidence to attend college in pursuit of her dreams. At the Midpoint, however, another low point tests the relationship. Grey sees her with another (younger) man across the college cafeteria. Without allowing her to explain the situation, he jumps to the conclusion it's only a matter of time before she dumps him for someone more interesting. To preempt seemingly certain heartbreak, he dumps her first. This is an even worse low than the break into Act Two. Emotionally there is much more on the line than testing where a relationship is headed. By now the couple have established a special bond. They mean something to each other, and this low is more than embarrassing. It's downright painful, and gives the reader a glimpse of how heartbreaking it would be for this couple to lose out on their happily ever after ending.

Meghan can't let him break her heart without providing a reason, but just as they work through Grey's issues, her insecurities about fitting into his academic world take their toll. At the New Direction event, she makes the decision to dump him for his own good. His stuck-up mother wholeheartedly agrees. He needs a fellow professional who can help advance his career, not a bright and sunny waitress who melts his heart. This is the worst low point of all, because by now the hero and heroine consciously understand they love each other and want to be with each other. The greatest love of their lives is at stake. But at least one of them is willing to sacrifice the relationship for the presumed better interest of the other.

At first blush Macomber's story seems to fly in the face of Gulino's and Snyder's theory that the Midpoint and its companion event should be opposites of each other. Actually, it's the exception that proves the rule. While the relationship hits new lows during both turning points, the core of the events are stark opposites. At the Midpoint the hero broke off the relationship, trying to protect himself from emotional pain. At the New Direction event, the relationship dynamics turn upside-down. The heroine breaks up with the hero, willingly inflicting emotional pain on herself in order to protect his career and position. So while the two events are both "lows," they are opposites in which character is driving each turning point and their purpose for doing so.

Low. Low. Low... Another low at the resolution would not only be predictable, but in a romance it would break the genre's contract with the reader. However, by now even the most diehard romance reader may be wondering how the writer can pull a happily ever after ending out of this. It may not even seem possible, because there has been no preview of it at the key turning points.

At the resolution, it's Grey's turn to pursue Meghan. He finds her in her apartment with not just another (younger) man, but a bunch of fellow students. Instead of letting his earlier insecurities resurge, he demonstrates confidence in their love and proposes marriage. Love triumphs on a high note, and the reader's satisfied.

What about a story with all "high" tension events, where the protagonist seems to get progressively closer and closer to success? To avoid predictability, the ending must necessarily be a "low." In cautionary tales, the final failure is depicted as either professional, physical, or emotional death. "What fruit had ye then in those things whereof ye are now ashamed? for the end of those things is death" (Romans 6:21, KJV). Even if the protagonist achieves what he set out to, the ultimate stakes are visited upon the unrepentant in some area of life that deprives him of deeper satisfaction.

In most stories, however, the protagonist eventually finds success on the other side of redemption. Regardless of genre, the journey is never easy. The path to a satisfying ending is mined with explosive tensions that blow the protagonist out of his comfort zone. The Midpoint ties together the fuse of anticipation that makes these three major turning points work.

The next chapter introduces the first half of the Midpoint, and how to tie the story threads together.

FURTHER READING

Suggestions to deepen your understanding of tension:

Cheryl St. John's *Writing with Emotion, Tension, and Conflict: Techniques for Crafting an Expressive and Compelling Novel.* Available in Kindle edition on Amazon and in print wherever books are sold.

Jessica Page Morrell's *Between the Lines: Master the Subtle Elements of Fiction Writing.* Chapter 3, "Cliffhangers & Thrusters." Chapter 16,

"Tension." Available in Kindle edition on Amazon and in print wherever books are sold.

Sherry Ellis and Laurie Lamson's *Now Write! Screenwriting: Screenwriting Exercises from Today's Best Writers and Teachers.* Chris Soth's chapter, "The Most Important Thing I Know and Teach." Available in ebook and print on Amazon and wherever books are sold.

Lydia Sharp's online article, "What's Your (Mid)Point?" Currently available on The Sharp Angle at: http://lydiasharp.blogspot.com/2010/11/whats-your-midpoint.html

Blake Snyder's *Save the Cat! The Last Book on Screenwriting You'll Ever Need.* Chapter 4, "Let's Beat it Out!" Available in Kindle edition on Amazon and in print wherever books are sold.

First Half of the Midpoint

Following the burning fuse to the central turning point marked on the terrain map, you machete aside vines and palmetto fronds to discover a small, enclosed clearing rising above the swampy muck. Smack in the middle sits a bomb the size of a boulder.

Palms growing slippery with sweat, you juggle various story threads, attempting to tie them into the central tension event. Relax. This is actually a lot simpler than it appears. It's just like tying together a pair of shoe laces into a bow. Except, of course, something is going to go *boom!* and hopefully that doesn't normally happen when you tie your shoes.

More than a fleeting moment or character point somewhere in the middle, the Midpoint is created from two major events sparking off each other like exposed wires. The effect on the protagonist is primal and jolting. He has no option but to respond with a decision to change either his goal or his way of pursuing it.

The first half of the Midpoint provides the stimulus to change. The second half kicks off the response.

An *event* simply means something significant happens that can't be taken back. If it's action, it can't be undone. If it's knowledge, it can't be unknown. That's why, although their internal ramifications are urgent and earthshaking, events are external and tangible to the physical senses. Naval-gazing on the beach doesn't cut it. The reader must see what specifically triggers the protagonist's transformation.

NYT bestselling novelist Jennifer Crusie wrote in an Argh Ink blog post, "External conflict is the only kind of conflict that moves plot. Internal conflict can demonstrate character growth but very rarely causes it." The power of the Midpoint is that it's both. External and internal conflicts cross paths and twist together, propelling plot *and* demonstrating character growth.

Stimulus. Response.

The first half of the Midpoint provides the stimulus by accomplishing **four** vital story functions:

- It shows the protagonist and the reader a preview of how the story *might* end. This can be positive or negative, true or false.
- It forces the protagonist to change the plan he executed at the beginning of Act Two.
- It shows the protagonist's flawed way of doing things letting him down in a big way.
- It reinforces and heightens the stakes by the death (professional, physical, or psychological) of someone/something important.

The more of these that make it onto the pages of the first-half Midpoint, the stronger the story will be. The fundamental functions of the Midpoint are explored in more detail in the chapters ahead. For now, let's look at how these functions take shape on the page.

After analyzing and taking apart hundreds of novels, movies, and television episodes to find out how they work, I've discovered **four** beats that empower the first half Midpoint to fulfill its dramatic functions. The term "beat" can mean different things, but for the purposes of this book, I'm going to use Dan Decker's definition in *Anatomy of a Screenplay*: "any Event, Decision, or Discovery that changes the *way* in which the characters pursue [their] objective." (185) *All four beats don't show up in the same Midpoint, but at least one of the four always does.* Every time. A bold claim, I know, but it's proven so invariably true I've yet to find an exception that made a story stronger and better.

Imagine the beats as loops on a bow. You can design a bow to have as many loops as you have room to handle, but to knot tightly together, it must have at least a minimum of one loop on each side. The left and right sides of the bow are like the first and second halves of the Midpoint.

In brief, the first-half Midpoint's four types of beats are:

- The protagonist ***Glimpses*** something.
- The protagonist's plan to achieve his goal is ***Cut Off***.
- A character is trapped or sets a ***Trap***.
- The protagonist is ***Attacked***.

The four beats are distinguished from each other primarily by how they are physically expressed in the story. For example, a death of some kind always occurs at the Midpoint. The protagonist may Glimpse death, his plan may be Cut Off by a death, he may be Trapped when someone dies, or he may be the target of a deadly Attack. Same Midpoint function, four different ways of expressing it on the page or screen.

Here's another example: the Midpoint always previews a possible positive or negative ending to the story. That function can be fulfilled by any of the four beats, but each of the four will express it differently on the page or screen. Allowing the protagonist to Glimpse a positive or negative version of the end is certainly a powerful and popular choice.

However, the savvy writer can try on the other three beats and get a feel for how they fit the story before settling on an option. He may even decide to combine a couple beats, as discussed later in the "Mix and Match" chapters.

How any particular beat looks in the story is limited only by the writer's imagination and the conventions of the genre. For example, an Attack may be as simple as a tongue-lashing or as high-tech as a military assault. A Glimpse may be as simple as the heroine putting on a pair of jeans, or as complex as revisiting childhood trauma. There are no limits on how the writer may interpret any of the beats.

The following chapters describe how each beat translates the essential functions of the Midpoint to page and screen. Multiple examples are provided demonstrating how other writers interpreted and utilized the beats to build strong Midpoints into stories from every genre. (Please be aware that examples do contain significant spoilers.)

FURTHER READING

Suggestions to deepen your understanding of the Midpoint:

Jeffrey Alan Schechter's *My Story Can Beat Up Your Story! Ten Ways to Toughen Up Your Screenplay.* Chapter 9, "I'm Not Afraid of the Dark." Available in Kindle edition on Amazon and in print wherever books are sold.

Christopher Vogler's *The Writer's Journey: Mythic Structure for Writers.* Chapter, "Stage Eight: The Ordeal." Available in print on Amazon and wherever books are sold.

Jim Butcher's online article, "The Great Swampy Middle." Currently available on his LiveJournal blog at: http://jimbutcher.livejournal.com/1865.html

"Quick Look"

Glimpse

Hallmark: *The protagonist experiences or hears about an experience mirroring a possible outcome to the story, either positive or negative.*

Use a Glimpse in the first half of your Midpoint to...

- Strengthen the protagonist's motivation by allowing him to taste and see the benefits of change.
- Make the protagonist reassess past or present relationships in a new light.
- Personalize the stakes.
- Bond characters closer together by revealing important backstory information.
- Force the protagonist to acknowledge flaws and weaknesses hampering his success and/or happiness.

Glimpse

The small clearing in the center of the Great Swampy Middle can be a magical oasis of unexpected wonder or a creepy cavern of unimaginable terror for the protagonist. Mainly it depends upon whether he requires a stick or a carrot to motivate him to take the next big step in his character arc.

Filmmaker, writer, and teacher Stanley D. Williams in *The Moral Premise* delves deeply into the conflict of issues spotlighted by the Midpoint, or as he calls it, the Moment of Grace. The Moral Premise, as described by Williams, pits a universal virtue against a universal vice. For example, forgiveness versus revenge. The story progresses through cause and effect, "reminding the characters of the reward that the virtue offers and the punishment that the vice threatens." (69)

The Midpoint represents the protagonist's deliberate shift from vice to virtue. Up until now, he pursued his goal using the vice. He probably didn't realize it was a vice. He was blind to its nastier qualities. At the Midpoint, he's forced to confront why this way of doing things has failed and why another way is better. "In some films the protagonist sees himself in a mirror (sometimes a real physical mirror, sometimes a symbolic one, and sometimes a moment of self-reflection), [and] recognizes the reality of his situation." (Williams 70)

He faces the truth of cause and effect, that his old way of doing things can only ever reap a harvest of defeat and failure. At the Midpoint, he accepts the thematic premise and from this moment on strives to apply the virtue toward obtaining his goal.

Writer and teacher James Scott Bell echoes Williams in his online article "The Magical Midpoint Moment," when he calls the Midpoint the "Look in the Mirror." Depending upon whether the story is plot-driven or character-driven, Bell says the protagonist will react to the Midpoint glimpse of himself in either one of two ways. "In a character-driven story, he looks at himself and wonders what kind of person he is." In plot-driven stories, "It's where the character looks at himself and considers the odds against him." Make no mistake, those odds mean nothing less than death, although the manifestation of his threatened demise "can be professional, physical, or psychological."

The protagonist glimpses a possible outcome and resolution, either positive or negative, pertaining to his goal and/or character growth. Emphasis on *possible*. It could be a glimpse of hope and beauty that inspires him to press on against the odds, or a glimpse of death and tragedy that challenges his commitment and tempts him to despair. Either way, it's not a done deal—yet.

Glimpses come in many shapes and fashions. A Glimpse can be an exchange of dialogue, such as a conversation revealing a previously-unconsidered perspective on things or describing something from the past or in the future. A Glimpse can also be an experience that happens to the protagonist in the present or that he witnesses occur to someone emotionally-connected to him.

Glimpses also can come from different directions. The protagonist may originate the Glimpse himself, only to have it reflected back at him in the looking glass of others' reactions. Or someone else may provide the Glimpse to the protagonist. The vital element here is that the protagonist must be present for the Glimpse to have an impact. Secondhand insight rarely imparts the conviction necessary to change on a fundamental level.

Almost always the Glimpse comes as a surprise, a life-altering shock to the system. Even if the protagonist seeks it out, he either isn't expecting it to be as sublimely good or as nightmarishly bad as it is. Which is why Glimpses most often occur in stories where the protagonist experiences a significant character arc and internal growth. The unexpectedness of the Glimpse jolts the rose-colored glasses off his face. It either gives him a clear perspective of how much he's already changed, how much he yet needs to change, or what will happen to himself and/or others if he rejects change. On the other hand, protagonists whose internal development focuses on recommitment to preexisting virtues in the face of temptation and hardship (for example, many series characters and John Wayne-type films) commonly rely upon other Midpoint beats.

ADVANCING CHARACTER GROWTH

The Glimpse could be the protagonist's experimenting with character growth, trying out a new attitude or behavior to see how it feels or works. He hasn't committed to it yet, but he's built up enough curiosity and courage to finally deviate from the norm. The biggest surprise is how much he enjoys this taste of a new lifestyle, behavior, or attitude. The joy and freedom is so addictive he can't ever go back to his old way of living with quite the same contentment as before.

In Debbie Macomber's sweet contemporary romance, *Rainy Day Kisses*, Susannah is a single career woman, driven in her focused pursuit of a choice promotion. When her new hunky, easygoing neighbor pitches in to help babysit her niece, her life path—as well as her heart—gets humorously derailed. At the 47.5% - 50% mark, she dresses for a date with the hero to fly kites in the park. For the first time *ever* she lets her hair down and wears jeans. Her sister gawks at this "glimpse" of a new Susannah who, also for the first time ever without being trapped into it, offers to babysit anytime.

ROLE REVERSAL

The Glimpse may enable the protagonist to simply see and/or experience someone in a new light, so that he reassesses wants and desires. While it doesn't necessarily change his perception of the past, it radically shifts his focus in the present, and thereby, the rest of the story. When character roles reverse, often goals must be adjusted accordingly.

As in the romantic comedy *While You Were Sleeping* (1995). Lonely Lucy (Sandra Bullock) fantasizes she's in love with a handsome stranger whose life she saved and who lies in a coma. Through a misunderstanding that quickly snowballs into a lie, his family adopts her as his fiancee, but Peter's brother isn't convinced. The antagonist to her external goal, Jack (Bill Pullman) does everything he can to protect his family and prove she's a fake. After overcoming all doubters, at the 47.5% - 50% mark, Lucy allows Jack to walk her home. They laugh together and share confidences about cherished dreams. It's her dream come true, everything she's always wanted from a loving relationship, but from a totally unexpected direction.

Up until this Glimpse, Lucy believed she wanted Peter. But seeing Jack in a new light, key roles in the story reverse. The antagonist becomes the love interest, and consequently now her goal must change.

Sometimes the Glimpse the protagonist receives makes him reassess everything that's happened before. What he thought was true might be exposed as all lies. Enemies might reveal themselves as true friends, and supposed friends turn out to be enemies manipulating the protagonist's deepest fears and needs.

In T. L. Hines' paranormal suspense *The Dead Whisper On*, the emotionally-isolated protagonist is recruited by her father's "ghost" into working for a shadowy organization to share the secrets of the next world with this one. Her altruistic missions give her lonely life meaning and direction, but also catapult her into a cat-and-mouse game with a menacing opponent named Keros. After a violent fight, at the 47.5% - 50% mark Candace awakens to find herself Keros's prisoner. Or is she? He claims to be her friend and to have rescued her from an organization devoted to furthering global crime and corruption. Those undercover cops she helped? Three serial killers. Her father's ghost? A demon from the underworld. Her Glimpse of the truth is a "step through the looking glass," and her perspective on everything changes at this pivotal moment.

DEVELOPING TENSION

While any of the Midpoint beats can successfully preview a possible outcome to the story, the Glimpse is tailor-made to fulfill this dramatic function. It focuses the protagonist's attention on consciously seeing what life could be like for themselves or a stakes character. Because of this event, the protagonist now has something even more valuable to fight for in the rest of the story.

As in Debbie Macomber's inspirational contemporary romance *The Gift of Christmas*. Ashley's grown up with a huge crush on her best friend's uncle, wealthy businessman Cooper. But her mother is his family's domestic servant, and despite an unmistakable mutual attraction, she feels their lives are destined to remain worlds apart. At the

47.5% - 50% mark, Ashley and Cooper are jointly tasked with babysitting a set of rambunctious boys, and Ashley tastes the joy of what family life with Cooper could be like.

Because Ashley experiences this happy Glimpse with Cooper, she knows what hope for the future tastes like when she's subsequently buffeted by conflict and self-doubt. There's always this moment to call back to, demonstrating to her what's possible and worth fighting for.

Glimpses can make the protagonist aware of possible outcomes and what's at stake in other ways. He may Glimpse what another character's life is like, or will be like, if he himself continues on his present course and rejects internal growth. Often the other character is the love interest in the main plot or a subordinate plot thread, but it may be a stakes character who's emotionally connected in some other way to the protagonist. Either way, the other character has to mean enough to the protagonist that the Glimpse is like a kick to the gut, awakening them to their responsibility for someone else's professional, physical, or emotional wellbeing.

In the romantic comedy-drama *People Will Talk* (1951), Dr. Noah Praetorius (Cary Grant) becomes entangled in a young unmarried student's private life when she attempts suicide after he diagnoses her pregnancy. He pursues Deborah (Jeanne Crain) to a farm in the country, in hopes of breaking the news to her kindly father and gaining support for her situation. But at the 47.5% - 50% mark, he Glimpses what her and her father's lives are like living with her strict, humorless uncle as "tax deductions." He becomes uncomfortably aware of the level of ignominy and disgrace his revelation, however well-intentioned, would reduce two gentle and dignified souls to. He holds his tongue.

BACKSTORY REVEALED

Backstory is an essential component of crafting three-dimensional characters. It's the part of the character's past that shaped who they are, defining wounds and flaws, prior to the beginning of the story. Everyone has a past that to some extent explains their present actions and attitudes. However, because backstory is about past events, it does nothing on its own to advance the present story. In fact, backstory stops the present story dead in its tracks. Which is why there are all sorts of prohibitions from experts and writing instructors on limiting significant backstory or information dumps in the first half of the story. Donald Maass in *Writing the Breakout Novel* says, "Breakout novelists hold it back for just the right moment, which can sometimes be quite late in the novel. That is especially true if backstory holds a buried secret." (191)

If a significant amount of backstory is necessary to build credibility into the story, the first-half Midpoint is a good place to consider revealing it as a Glimpse. The key is to make it about more than revealing the backstory alone. It needs to serve a purpose in the *now* of the story.

The character has kept this information private for a good reason. Their secret makes them vulnerable. But now they are willing to trade it as a token of trust and faith in an important relationship. They've come to want something more than self-protection. Now they want closeness, connection, and understanding. Backstory at the first-half Midpoint comes as a discovery of new knowledge that immediately raises the stakes. It evokes an awareness in reader and character alike that there is much more to win or lose than previously imagined.

As in Sara Mitchell's historical romance *Shenandoah Home.* Garnet is an eccentric backwoods artist, whose extremely shy disposition puts her at uncomfortable odds with a growing reputation and demand for her work. Sloan comes to her Shenandoah haven, fleeing family, fortune, and fame as a brilliant physician, in order to escape a tragic past. When Garnet's injured rescuing a wild animal, Sloan is compelled to once again pick up his doctor's bag, if only this once. At the 47.5% - 50% mark, while removing Garnet's stitches, Sloan encourages her to tell him why she lives in such mortal fear. Slowly, bit by bit, she allows him to Glimpse her terror when, as a teenager, she was nearly raped by a gang of men burying a body in the woods—men who threatened to find her one day and kill her whole family.

This Glimpse of Garnet's backstory explains her reticent nature, but more importantly for advancing the present story, it accomplishes so much more. Sharing her secret with the romantic interest/antagonist bonds them together, *and* increases the stakes by revealing a clear and present danger to herself and other beloved supporting characters.

STRENGTHS AND WEAKNESSES

Heading into the Midpoint, the protagonist thinks he knows everything he needs to know about his own vulnerabilities and the forces arrayed against him. Sun Tzu (c. 6BC) said in chapter three of *The Art of War*, "...If you know your enemies and know yourself, you will not be imperiled in a hundred battles; if you do not know your enemies but do know yourself, you will win one and lose one; if you do not know your enemies nor yourself, you will be imperiled in every single battle."

Of course, his character arc is incomplete and he's unwittingly lining up to hit a major bump in the road at the Midpoint. That bump knocks the rose-colored glasses off his face, and he Glimpses the truth about his own weaknesses and/or the antagonist's superior strengths.

The protagonist may Glimpse his greatest fear, forcing him to confront the fact that his flaw, instead of a strength protecting him from pain and mistakes like he once believed, is actually his biggest barrier to happiness. This is often a "false Glimpse," as what he thinks he sees isn't the whole picture or is taken out of context, but nevertheless it forces him to honestly reassess his values and weaknesses.

As in Debbie Macomber's sweet contemporary romance *The Way to a Man's Heart.* Grey is a stuffy literature professor, who begins to experience life outside the ivy walls when his lively literary discussions with younger and vivacious waitress Meghan develops into a relationship. He encourages her to pursue her passion and enroll at his college. But at the 47.5% - 50% mark, he spots her across the school cafeteria chatting and laughing with a group of fellow students—and one youthful, handsome student in particular. He sees her bright future ahead of her—a future he doesn't fit into. Faced with his own flaws (stuffy, staid, uninteresting, etc...), his jealousy quickly crumbles into insecurity and despair, and he calls her up to break off the romance without giving her a chance to explain.

Grey's Glimpse of a possible negative future outcome exposes his flaw to his own eyes for the liability it is. Behaviors and attitudes he previously considered strengths supporting his goal are now weaknesses holding him back from the happiness he wants. As bitter as the truth is, it's a necessary test of his character. Does he want happiness more than he wants his flaws?

The protagonist may believe he's come to learn and fully comprehend the villain's power and influence, his plans and the scope of his designs, only to Glimpse how shockingly wrong he was. The villain is more powerful, more ahead of the game, than the protagonist had any concept of.

As in Robert Heinlein's science fiction classic *The Puppet Masters.* After aliens invade earth and take government agent Sam Cavanaugh hostage to their tyrannical mind control, he escapes with the hard-earned conviction he's seen the dark side and lived to warn the world about "the masters." Government response moves too slowly for some already infected areas, though, whose residents never receive the public warning messages. Mere hours ahead of a full-force military strike against alien strongholds, Sam goes on a scouting mission to presumably "safe" Kansas City. At the 47.5% - 50% mark, he gets an up-close-and-personal look at the large-population metropolis, which is completely under the control of the alien masters. He realizes to his horror that the mighty US military forces gathering to clean up the residue of the alien invasion are in fact hopelessly outnumbered and heading for certain disaster.

Protagonists aren't the only characters who can Glimpse the truth about an opponent's resources. The antagonist/villain may Glimpse a truth or vulnerability the protagonist is unwilling to face or desperate to hide, and confront the protagonist about it. Acknowledging a goal, alliance, or personal weakness to an opponent usually carries high stakes, either emotional, physical, or both.

As in the classic romantic thriller *Notorious* (1946). Government agent Devlin (Cary Grant) recruits notorious party girl Alicia (Ingrid Bergman) to infiltrate a German spy ring in South America, using any and every wile at her disposal. Neither counts on falling madly in love, or the pain and betrayal they inflict on each other when Alicia pursues her mission to seduce Alex Sebastian (Claude Raines). At the 47.5% - 50% mark, Alex spies Alicia and Devlin meeting at the race track, and confronts her about what he Glimpsed. It looks to him as though she is in love with Devlin. Aware Alex's suspicions are dangerous to her as well as the mission, she denies the truth. Not easily dissuaded from the evidence of his eyes, Alex challenges her to prove to him Devlin means nothing to her.

FURTHER READING

Suggestions to deepen your understanding of the Glimpse beat:

Stanley D. William's *The Moral Premise: Harnessing Virtue & Vice for Box Office Success.* Chapter 5, "The Structure of the Moral Premise." Available in Kindle edition on Amazon and in print wherever books are sold.

Dara Marks' *Inside Story: The Power of the Transformational Arc.* Chapter 8, "Act II—Part One: What Goes Up..." Available in print on Dara Marks' website.

Blake Snyder's *Save the Cat! Strikes Back: More Trouble for Screenwriters to Get Into... and Out Of.* Chapter 3, "All Laid Out... and Nowhere to Go." Available in Kindle edition on Amazon and in print wherever books are sold.

"Quick Look"

Double Glimpse

Hallmark: *The protagonist encounters back-to-back experiences and/or hears about more than one experience mirroring a possible outcome to the story, either positive or negative.*

Use a Double Glimpse in the first half of your Midpoint to...

- Impress upon the protagonist more than one angle of a possible outcome.
- Throw the protagonist's external and internal goals into conflict.
- Frame personalized stakes in a larger context.
- Contrast true and false perceptions.
- Strengthen motivation by bonding the protagonist and love interest together in a "big love scene."

Double Glimpse

After facing the rigors of trekking deep into the heart of the Everglades, the protagonist may doubt the evidence of his own eyes at the Midpoint. A hard or challenging truth can be dismissed as a mirage or hallucination brought on by thirst or fatigue. Even a vision of something hoped for may seem too good to be true and not dared to be believed. When reason gets in the way of reality, it's time for reality to double down.

The Glimpse is such a powerful character transformation tool that it can occur in pairs at the Midpoint for maximum dramatic impact. When that happens, I call it the Double Glimpse. Though it fulfills in every way the dramatic purposes of a single Glimpse, double Glimpses earn special mention by themselves. 1 Glimpse + 1 Glimpse always equals more than the sum of its parts.

Each Glimpse commonly gets it own scene, so that it can be fully developed and the character allowed to appreciate its full effect. Therefore, Double Glimpses rarely occur in short novels. They need the extra room of at least a medium-length or longer page count. Remember, we're dealing with 2.5% here. In a category romance novel of around 180 pages, that's only about 4 pages—great for a Glimpse, but probably too tight for a successful double. A single title of around 350 pages, on the other hand, has about nine pages to comfortably pack in that one-two punch.

Percentages and page counts aside, a Double Glimpse is a balancing act of dramatic needs. Each Glimpse comes as a shock, a surprise, so focus and pacing is important. (It's hard to be surprised in slow motion.) At the same time, without descending into naval-gazing, the character and reader must be given time to absorb the ramifications and consequences of each Glimpse before the next one occurs. It's like being surprised by a flashbulb at a birthday party. The last image you see is burned onto your retinas. Likewise, the character's vision has to clear a bit, however briefly, before the next flash goes off in order for him to recognize what he's seeing.

DOUBLE EXPOSURE

Sometimes the protagonist needs to Glimpse a possible outcome from more than one angle before they're impressed. The antagonist is usually more than willing to step up to the challenge. In romances, this is commonly expressed as a "big love scene," regardless of whether the heat level is mildly sweet or scorching hot.

As in Lisa Kleypas's sexy contemporary romance *Smooth-Talking Stranger*. Advice-columnist Ella's search for the unidentified father of her sister's baby leads her mistakenly to the doorstep of a wealthy Texan businessman. Jack's capable and willing assistance with everything from the paternity search to housing to baby care trips every alarm commitment-phobic Ella possesses. Even more, his determined pursuit of her heart dangerously upsets the equanimity she once shared with her no-strings, AWOL boyfriend. Dead on her feet from the exhaustion of unexpected, full-time childcare, at the 47.5% - 50% mark, Ella allows Jack to escort her to her apartment. He sets out to prove to her he knows how to put her first, and gives her a goodnight kiss loaded with such powerful fireworks that she orgasms. That's Glimpse number one—an experience giving Ella a small taste of what lovemaking with Jack might be like. Later, Ella meets Jack for lunch to discuss the paternity search. He seduces her without even touching her by describing in detail his version of a perfect day. This is Glimpse number two—dialogue giving Ella a clear view of how enchanting life with Jack might be. Emotionally stricken, she realizes the stakes have escalated. She's in real danger of falling in love and getting her heart broken.

COMPETING GOALS

A double Glimpse can throw the protagonist's external and internal goals into conflict by tantalizing him with two highly desirable but irreconcilable possible outcomes. Naturally, this raises the stakes and places the reins of the story firmly in the hands of the protagonist, whose decision will determine the direction of the rest of the story.

As in the adventure movie *The Raiders of the Lost Ark* (1981). Archaeologist Indiana Jones (Harrison Ford) races against Nazis around the globe for the Ark of the Covenant. Believing his first love has been killed, he focuses all his efforts on finding the Ark ahead of his arch rival, Belloq, and Hitler's SS. At the 47.5% - 50% mark, Indy uses the Staff of Ra in the Map Room where a brilliant flash of light pinpoints the exact location of the Ark. His external goal is within sight! (First Glimpse.) Then he stumbles into a tent and finds Marian, bound and gagged, but very much alive. His internal goal, once believed irredeemably lost, is also within sight! (Second Glimpse.) But now he must choose, because he can't have both.

STAKES

Stakes are made all the more visceral for reader and characters alike when they are both personalized and contextualized. *Showing* either positive or negative consequences directly associated with specific actions personalizes the stakes. *Telling* either positive or negative consequences directly associated with specific actions puts the stakes in context of a larger perspective. Double Glimpses can be one of the clever writer's ways to both show *and* tell what's at stake.

Consider Ella in Kleypas's *Stranger.* The first Glimpse Jack gives her is experiential. It engages all her senses. It's in the present time of the story. It *shows* Ella one specific angle of a potential outcome to the story. (The sexual part of Ella and Jack happily together in a serious committed relationship.) Anything the character is shown, they then know to be true. All that's left is to deal with it. But a particularly stubborn character might choose to compartmentalize that event or even isolate it as a one-off thing. Maybe Ella rationalizes she responded to Jack's kiss the way she did simply because she's stressed and missing her boyfriend.

The second Glimpse Jack gives her is via dialogue. There's no touching, and though the sensory perception is sensual, it's also subtle and minimal. The dialogue is focused not on the present, but on the future. It *tells* Ella another highly specific angle of the same potential outcome to the story. (The sharing-life part of Ella and Jack happily together in a serious relationship.) Telling provides the character with scope and context (for example, describing a whole day is more comprehensive than a single kiss), while also testing their ability or willingness to trust. While the character might have been doubtful or demanded proof earlier in the story, placing their trust in someone at the Midpoint is an important sign of internal growth. When Jack describes his idea of a perfect day, even though she's never experienced it with him, Ella has no trouble at this point believing him.

TRUE OR FALSE?

It's a good rule of thumb that if the Glimpse is *shown* and the protagonist personally experiences it, then generally it's true. Because it's true, the character is compelled to adapt his beliefs and behaviors to this new truth. In other words, the character makes significant advancement in his internal growth. The exception proving this rule is the "incomplete Glimpse," when the reader is given superior knowledge and knows in advance the protagonist isn't seeing the whole picture.

As in Debbie Macomber's *The Way to a Man's Heart.* The reader experienced the cafeteria scene up-close-and-personal with the heroine before the hero walks in and Glimpses her with a younger man. He takes what he observes from a distance out of context, without knowing all the facts. So the reader knows it's a false Glimpse appearing real.

On the other hand, if a Glimpse is shown, and both reader and character believe it to be true, only for it later to be proven false, the reader will feel cheated and betrayed.

If the protagonist *tells* a Glimpse to another character, it's false. The simple reason is that the protagonist has yet to complete his character growth. He's probably not deliberately lying, but he's unaware he's missing key pieces of the puzzle. This is also true for flashbacks or backstory revealed by the protagonist as a Glimpse at the Midpoint.

For example, in Sara Mitchell's *Shenandoah Home,* the heroine confides a horrible event from her childhood to the hero. While the details are strictly true, her perception of what it means to her is false in a significant way. It formed a specific erroneous belief that shaped her actions ever since, just as in James Oliver Curwood's *The Flaming Forest,* when the protagonist's belief in a fugitive's guilt (while strictly true) drives him unwittingly to promote a terrible injustice.

If the antagonist *tells* a Glimpse to the protagonist, generally it's true. That's because the antagonist's role is to provoke and challenge the protagonist to change, and up until the Midpoint the protagonist was believing a lie anyway. A false Glimpse from the antagonist at this point would only reinforce the internal status quo. So the antagonist tries to break through that lie by showing and/or telling him the truth about how things were, are, or can be.

If the morally-evil villain *tells* a Glimpse to the protagonist, generally it's false. (While on the other hand, the villain is quite likely to *show* off his true power.) A villain's role is to defeat the protagonist, and sometimes that means at the Midpoint trying to intimidate him into giving up. The protagonist is challenged to grow by the simple fact that if he doesn't change enough to see through the falsehood, he'll probably die or be killed. The exception that proves the rule is when the reader has already experienced the event and knows in advance the villain is describing something that's true.

As in the romantic thriller *Notorious* (1946). The audience experienced Alicia's heartbreak during her meeting with Devlin, her anguish at his rejection, and her tears at his refusal to admit his love for her. When Alex tells her he Glimpsed them together, and it looked like she's in love with Devlin, the audience doesn't have to take his word for it. They *know* experientially it's true, despite her denials, and fully appreciate the danger it represents to her life and heart.

Sometimes the Double Glimpse pits something true against something false, heightening stakes while also laying bare the protagonist's internal conflict. For truth to win out over falsehood in this showdown, the true Glimpse needs to be more visceral, more powerful, and more convincing than the false Glimpse. That means the true Glimpse should be experienced or *shown*, while the false Glimpse is *told*. Remember, showing is believing, as far as the reader is concerned. To sustain reader identification, it should be that way for the protagonist and other characters, too.

To create the most tension, *tell* the false Glimpse first, then *show* the true Glimpse. Why does it work better in that order? For one thing, it builds intensity from lesser to greater, because telling is always less intense than showing. Another reason is the reader has more time to worry (which is a good thing!) if it looks like the protagonist is committing to a falsehood before he has a chance to experience the truth.

As in James Oliver Curwood's *The Flaming Forest.* When Royal Canadian Mounted Policeman David Carrigan is shot and injured in pursuit of a notorious murderer, he's nursed back to health by the beautiful Marie-Anne. She holds him captive pending the return of the man she claims as her husband, the renowned St. Pierre, whom David believes either knows where Black Roger is hiding or may be the villain himself. Recovered from his wounds, at the 47.5% - 50% mark, David attempts to win Marie-Anne's cooperation by recounting a horrifically detailed account of Black Roger's crimes. That's Glimpse number one—dialogue giving Marie-Anne insight into the past as seen through the unforgiving eyes of the law, and also suggesting a possible violent and bloody future if Black Roger is not captured, since he's crazy enough to kill again. However, this Glimpse is false, because David doesn't know the whole story, and Marie-Anne reacts differently than he expected. Later, she accompanies David on a walk through the woods, and while crossing a stream, for several precious moments she's clasped in his embrace. That's Glimpse number two—a rapturous experience revealing a potential future outcome. (David and Marie-Anne together happily ever after.) This is a true Glimpse of his heart and deepest longings that rocks him to his core.

TRIPLE GLIMPSES

Triple Glimpses are also not rare, but typically occur in epics or stories with a large cast of characters. The Glimpses are usually shared or distributed among several key characters, with at least one Glimpse (the biggest or most important) reserved for the protagonist.

As in J.R.R. Tolkien's classic fantasy *The Hobbit.* Bilbo accompanies a group of dwarves on an adventure through treacherous and enemy-filled terrain to wrest control of a fabulous treasure from the clutches of a fearsome dragon. At the 47.5% – 50% mark, they are lost and starving to death in the poisonous maze of Mirkwood Forest. Bilbo climbs a tree to gain some bearings on their location, and Glimpses nothing but endless trees in all directions. Unknown to him (but revealed to the reader), they are very near the edge of the forest, but because of a hill he cannot see it. Thus, when he returns to the dwarves, it's with the unwittingly false report that there is no way out. That's the first Glimpse, a significant false one delivered by the protagonist revealing a very bad potential outcome to their quest. (That they all die on the journey and never make it to Smaug's Mountain.) Haunted by hunger and despair, Bilbo and the dwarves begin to dream of sumptuous, all-you-can-eat feasts. These additional false Glimpses torment them, fomenting strife, and nearly drive them mad. (Internal conflict laid bare.) Finally, they spot wood elves feasting in the forest. But when the dwarves attempt to approach and beg sustenance, the lights go out and every delicious crumb disappears. This third Glimpse is a double-edged sword. The elves and the food are real and true, but the dwarves' inability to partake of it portends a false outcome by reinforcing the possibility that none of them will make it out of Mirkwood alive.

FURTHER READING

More suggestions to deepen your understanding of the Glimpse beat:

James Scott Bell's *Write Your Novel from the Middle: A New Approach for Plotters, Pantsers and Everyone in Between*, available in Kindle edition and print on Amazon.

Rob Tobin's *The Screenwriting Formula: Why It Works and How to Use It.* Chapter 11, "Act Two, Part One." Available in print on Amazon and wherever books are sold.

"Quick Look"

Cut Off

Hallmark: *The protagonist is blocked from continuing on his chosen path, and in order to advance, must change direction.*

Use a Cut Off in the first half of your Midpoint to...

- Make the protagonist reassess internal values and priorities associated with a new course of action.
- Establish a time limit or ticking clock.
- Break up an important relationship so the protagonist will be compelled to work at overcoming his flaws in order to reconcile.
- Test the protagonist's commitment to his goal by providing him an excuse to quit.
- Shift the nature and direction of antagonistic forces arrayed against the protagonist.

Cut Off

Hacking his way through the Great Swampy Middle, the protagonist sees a clearing in the very center. Believing the hardest part is over, he heaves a sigh of relief and barrels ahead, only to ram head-first into a wall camouflaged by moss and vines. A hundred feet high and just as thick, it blocks his path as far as the eye can see. His only recourse, if he's truly committed to advancing the story, is to change direction and find another way.

Late screenwriting guru Syd Field was a modern champion of the three-act structure, and over thirty years after their initial publication, his screenwriting books are still considered foundational references. Perhaps the first to identify the Midpoint by name, he is certainly the most famous to coin the term. In *The Screenwriter's Workbook*, Field defines the Midpoint as "some kind of incident, episode, or event that shifts the action into another direction." (126) It's a vital link, a bridge, between the first and second halves of Act Two.

While Field explores examples, he skimps on detailing what *kind* of incident, episode, or event distinguishes the Midpoint from other incidents, episodes, or events in the rest of the story. Nevertheless, he touches on a basic truth. The Midpoint swivels the protagonist's path in a new direction in pursuit of his goal.

Screenwriting consultant and teacher Linda Seger in her classic *Making a Good Script Great, Revised & Expanded Second Edition* reiterates Field's assertion of the Midpoint as a change in direction "while still keeping the overall focus of Act Two which has been determined by the [break into Act Two]." (35)

Writing teacher and award-winning mystery writer Carolyn Wheat in *How to Write Killer Fiction* characterizes the Midpoint in terms of mystery novels, but her insights are applicable to all genres. "Violence or danger to the detective in and of itself is *not* really a Midpoint event if all it does is add more pressure without changing the direction of the investigation." While this is a popular place in mysteries and thrillers for a body to drop, especially if it belongs to the prime suspect, it's only truly dramatic if it means something more than wringing a gasp from the reader. "The essence of the Midpoint—of the shift from [the first half of Act Two to the second half of Act Two]—is that the detective must double back, must rethink, must re-examine everything he's already done." (68-70)

In the first half of the story, the protagonist pursues a goal. He has a plan, and follows it with limited success. He may even think by this point that he's got victory in sight. He thinks he knows everything he needs to know about the antagonist/villain, when—suddenly!—he's cut off at the pass. The antagonist has seized the initiative, or perhaps been lying in wait all along. If he's going to press on, he must reassess what he's doing that's working and what's not. The only option left him is to change direction, which often involves a reorganization of values or priorities.

Up until now the obstacles he encountered could be pushed through with a doubling-down of will or determination. Not this time. No amount of resolve can move the wall suddenly looming up in front of his face. The protagonist is the irresistible force, the Cut Off is the immoveable object. Which one is going to give? Well, the protagonist can't give up, or else the story ends half way. But neither can the immoveable object politely move out of the way, else the protagonist reaches his goal without having to grow or change.

The Cut Off tests the protagonist's commitment to his goal, while simultaneously challenging him to abandon ways and means that would never—could never—enable him to ultimately succeed. The Cut Off is so complete that there is no going forward... unless he changes direction.

CUT OFF AT THE PASS... LITERALLY

One of the most classic and straightforward expressions of the Cut Off is a physical wall or tangible obstacle blocking the protagonist's path. It could be a firewall in a cyber thriller. Or a flood-swollen stream in a western. Regardless, while it blocks the protagonist's progress in the external plot, it forces him to reassess internal values and priorities.

As in Daniel Defoe's classic man-against-nature tale, *Robinson Crusoe*. The famous castaway builds a canoe to scout and eventually escape the deserted island he's been shipwrecked on for years, and sets sail. Except at the 47.5% - 50% mark he finds a solid wall of rock jutting out into the ocean, blocking his way around the island. He's literally Cut Off. Attempting to go around it, he's caught in a powerful current and swept out to sea where his priorities abruptly flip. Instead of wanting nothing so much as getting off his island prison, he finds himself wanting nothing so much as returning to the safety and sustenance it suddenly represents.

Sometimes a ticking clock coupled with an obvious and tangible fork in the road pressures the protagonist to change direction on his own initiative. He knows clearly what's at stake by now. The first half of the story has lifted the veil from his eyes, and he can no longer delude himself that the path he's on will lead to a satisfying resolution. His best or perhaps only chance at true happiness or at least a better life is within reach. But only if he Cuts Off the old support systems for his flawed behavior and turns aside from the primrose path of moral failure. It's a big step, and he may not be sure he's up to the task.

As in the classic romantic movie *An Affair to Remember* (1957). An international playboy (Cary Grant) engaged to a wealthy socialite meets and flirts aboard ship with the mistress (Deborah Kerr) of a successful businessman. Both have a well-developed appreciation for limited responsibilities and the finer things in life. Slowly their shipboard fling turns into a deep and true love. By then their arrival in New York (and subsequent reunion with their significant others) is imminent. At the 47.5% - 50% mark, the end of their voyage means Cutting Off their love affair, unless they are willing to turn their entire lives in a new direction, away from the security they've enjoyed. It's clear to them that their love for each other is their only chance at genuine happiness and real personal dignity. What isn't clear at all is whether either of them is strong enough to Cut Off the comfortable lifestyles they're addicted to in exchange for a path forged from hard work and commitment.

BIG BREAKUP

In romances, this is a favorite spot for the Big Breakup event. Just when the relationship seemed to be coming up roses, it's abruptly Cut Off. The underlying reason depends upon whether it's the protagonist or the antagonist initiating the breakup. If it's the protagonist cutting off the relationship, then it's probably because of latent fears and flaws rising to the surface and scaring the stuffing out of him.

As in Debbie Macomber's contemporary romance *The Way to a Man's Heart*. Staid literature professor Grey encourages lively waitress Meghan to pursue her dream of attending college. At the 47.5% - 50% mark, he Glimpses her across the school cafeteria chatting with friends—a young, handsome friend in particular. All Grey's fears and insecurities flare to life. He's forced to admit to himself that his old stuffy ways can't win the heroine's love, but though his flaws have lost their previous luster, he feels unable to change. Seeking to avoid the inevitable pain of her throwing him over for a younger, more interesting man, Grey preemptively breaks up with her.

The protagonist may *try* to give up his goal and quit, but that doesn't mean he gets a free pass to walk out of the story and back to his old life. In the second part of the Midpoint yet to come, the antagonist won't let him, and he realizes he's passed the point of no return. But right now, at the Cut Off, quitting may *seem* like a legitimate, although profoundly unsatisfying, option that he's willing to consider. This dramatically demonstrates to the reader not only the stakes involved (especially what he's in danger of throwing away), but also how deeply his flaws are rooted in his personality, to the point the protagonist truly doesn't believe change is possible—yet.

If the antagonist initiates the Big Breakup event here, it's because the protagonist has not yet earned his happily ever after. Being Cut Off from some cherished aspect of the relationship, or the relationship as a whole, awakens the protagonist to his flaws. He may have believed the relationship was secure, only to discover he was ignoring a vital element within his control that must be dealt with first in order to win happiness.

As in James Oliver Curwood's bestselling historical romance *The Alaskan*. Alan reserves his passions for his ranch and revenge against his father's murderer. He has no special interest in women, until a beautiful runaway en route to Alaska selects him as her escort aboard the *Nome*. Mary enchants and frustrates him, but when he rejects her mysterious request for aid and she's later declared lost overboard, guilt nearly drives him mad. He realizes he loved her, and romantic fantasies build in his fevered mind until he arrives at his remote ranch, where he finds Mary miraculously waiting for him. Overcome, he sweeps her into his arms and kisses her. At the 47.5% - 50% mark, she firmly cuts off his amorous fantasies. She didn't travel all this great distance for *that*. She came because she believed from the first he was a man who could be relied on, who could be trusted. So even while their friendship resumes, his romantic hopes are ruthlessly dashed. He hasn't earned her love—yet.

ANTAGONISTS HAVE FRIENDS, TOO

Sometimes the protagonist's path to resolving his situation with the antagonist is Cut Off by a supporting character strongly allied with the antagonist. This may take the form of revealing key information previously unknown to the protagonist. The other character may even be completely unaware of the significance of what he's done, but the protagonist knows all too well it means he must change his plans.

As in the romantic movie *People Will Talk* (1951). When an unwed mother (Jeanne Crain) insists she would rather kill herself than admit her shame to her beloved father, Dr. Noah Praetorius (Cary Grant) plans a direct appeal to the man himself. But after meeting her gentle father, whose dignified failures in life pale upside his supreme regard for his daughter, at the 47.5% - 50% mark, Noah admits to himself what he intended to do is going to be a lot harder than he thought. He can't bring himself to tell her father the truth any more than she could. He's

Cut Off, and must dig deep down within himself to find another solution for the situation.

CONFLICT GETS PERSONAL

The Cut Off frequently denotes a change or shift in the nature of the antagonist and the direction of attack. For the first half of the story, obstacles are specific to the plot, but often personal to the protagonist only on the level of who he is professionally or socially. After the Midpoint, the obstacles become simultaneously universal (issues common to humanity) *and* personal to the protagonist on the deeper spiritual level of values and beliefs.

As in the movie version of Margaret Mitchell's classic historical epic *Gone With the Wind*. For the first half of the story, Scarlett O'Hara's biggest obstacle has been war, war, war! The war takes all the available beaus away, and her beloved Ashley, too. War traps her in a burning city with Melanie and a new baby. War decimates Tara and the whole South. But while war is highly specific to the plot of the story, and Scarlett suffers directly and personally because of it, her struggle centered on who she is: a spoiled Southern belle fighting for survival. Then at the 47.5% - 50% mark in the movie, Lee surrenders the Southern armies to Grant, abruptly cutting off the war. Everyone is relieved, jubilant.

When a significant source of antagonism is unexpectedly Cut Off, the protagonist may erroneously assume happy days are here at last. He thinks he won't have to change, after all. But it's a false victory that doesn't last. The source of antagonism is not over, merely changing direction, metamorphosing into something more deeply personal and closer to home. As soon as Scarlett begins making plans for a post-war future, Reconstruction rears its evil head as carpetbaggers invade the ravaged South. Not just anonymous carpetbaggers, either. The fiendish overseer her late mother sent packing years ago returns with a grudge and power to flaunt. The conflict abruptly deepens, targeting the values Scarlett holds dear in Tara and her instinctive, tenacious belief in the personal freedom that private land represents.

FURTHER READING

Suggestions to deepen your understanding of the Cut Off beat:

Billy Mernit's *Writing the Romantic Comedy.* Chapter 6, "Structuring Conflict." Available in print on Amazon and wherever books are sold.

Peter Dunne's *Emotional Structure: Creating the Story Beneath the Plot.* Chapter 11, "The Journey Through the Middle." Available in Kindle edition on Amazon or in print from sellers of used books.

"Quick Look"

Trap

Hallmark: *The antagonist plans, lays, or springs a trap on the protagonist, closing off all options. Or, the protagonist plans, lays, or springs a trap targeting the villain, but his flaw causes him to miss the mark.*

Use a Trap in the first half of your Midpoint to...

- Give the antagonist the upper hand by discovering and exploiting the protagonist's vulnerability (often associated with a relationship).
- Demonstrate the protagonist's courage, commitment, or arrogance if he walks into the Trap with his eyes open.
- Flip the balance of power between the protagonist and antagonist.
- Raise the stakes by putting a love interest in jeopardy.
- Tighten the screws on the protagonist with an impossible moral dilemma.

Trap

The protagonist steps into the clearing at the Midpoint. This is the place for the rendezvous, the big confrontation, but the antagonist is nowhere in sight. The hairs on the back of his neck come to attention, but he can't pinpoint a tangible reason for alarm. Everything seems quiet, calm, and peaceful. Too peaceful. He takes a cautious step forward. Suddenly, the ground drops out from under him, and he falls. A steel cage clangs shut around him. He's trapped!

The Midpoint Trap not only throws an insurmountable roadblock in front of the protagonist's forward progress, but also closes off any attempt to retreat or change direction. There's nowhere else to go. All options are denied. It looks like there is no way out and this is the end. He's reached the end of his rope—that rope being his old flawed way of doing things.

Traps turn up the heat and pressure on the protagonist, until the dross of flawed beliefs crumble away to ashes and only golden truth remains. For the first half of the story, he tried doing things the easy way or at least the way familiar to him. The Trap reveals that the old behavior not only doesn't work, but actually makes him vulnerable. He's forced to face the fact that instead of making him safer or more successful as he long believed, his flaw or fear has led him into a dead end and his own destruction.

GOTCHA!

The protagonist isn't the only character impacted by the Midpoint, however. Blake Snyder in *Save the Cat Strikes Back!* addresses the antagonist's role and perspective. "The Midpoint is... where the secret power or flaw of a hero, or his role in besting the Bad Guy, is discovered... It's also where, if the hero is hiding, or his location is unknown, 'the Bad Guy learns the hero's whereabouts.'" (52)

This is exactly what happens in C.S. Lewis's classic Narnia fantasy *The Lion, the Witch, and the Wardrobe.* During the London blitz, the Pevensie children (Peter, Susan, Edmund, and Lucy) discover a magic wardrobe that ushers them into a magical world. Frozen in perpetual winter under the tyrannical rule of the White Queen, the inhabitants' only hope lies in the return of her sworn enemy, Aslan the lion, to depose her. At the 47.5% - 50% mark, Edmund treks alone to the evil White Queen's forbidding castle to betray the location of his siblings and Aslan. She immediately launches her forces to Trap them.

The element of betrayal injected into the Trap is especially potent, coupling internal pain and disillusionment with external threat and imminent danger. Suddenly the protagonists are forced to reassess everything they know about the relationship. The closer the relationship, the worse the peril, the higher the stakes.

The Trap may be more about the villain isolating the protagonist's soft spot and planning how to lure him into the Trap than actually springing it. Granting the reader a position of superior knowledge is a classic and proven suspense tool. Privy to the villain's plan, the reader's tension mounts as he watches the protagonist unwittingly step closer and closer to disaster.

As in the movie *The Adventures of Robin Hood* (1938). The noble robber (Errol Flynn) brazenly foils and mocks evil Prince John (Claude Raines) and his thieving allies time and again. He even captures a rich caravan guarded personally by Sir Guy and the Sheriff of Nottingham. After their release, at the 47.5% - 50% mark, the two henchmen return to Prince John and report witnessing Robin and Maid Marian walking together in the woods. They suspect love is in the air. The sheriff proposes a plan to Trap the outlaw bowman by appealing to both his ego and his heart. They will host an archery tournament, with Maid Marian personally presenting the prize.

The most primal and straightforward expression of the Trap is where the villain simply chases the protagonist until there's nowhere left to run. The protagonist is trapped, waiting to die.

As in Suzanne Collins' dystopian fantasy *The Hunger Games*. When Katniss takes her sister's place in the gladiatorial Games, she comes to believe she's got an ally in fellow tribute Peeta. But when the Games begin, Peeta stuns her by banding together with a gang of rival tributes to hunt her down and kill her. At the 47.5% - 50% mark, Katniss can run and hide no longer. Surrounded, she finds herself literally Trapped up in a tree, awaiting the dawn and a violent death.

TURNING THE TABLES

Sometimes walking into the villain's Trap with both eyes open is the best way for the protagonist to unmask or identify his true opponent. The intended fly may commandeer the spider's web for his own purposes, perhaps tweaking it to Trap the villain himself.

As in the James Bond movie *Dr. No* (1962). When rocket launches on the East Coast are mysteriously disrupted and a British agent disappears in Jamaica, 007 becomes embroiled in a tangled tropical web involving the CIA, mineral samples, and a wealthy recluse. Surviving several attempts on his life, 007 is on alert for another when a femme fatale lures him to her bungalow for a sexy tryst. At the 47.5% - 50% mark, he foils her attempts to hold him there for the evening and hands her over to the authorities. Then he sets about re-staging the bungalow as a Trap, and sits back to wait for the would-be assassin's anticipated arrival.

The protagonist himself may lay a Trap at the Midpoint for the antagonist. He's had half the story to study and learn his adversary's ways and means. He believes he's got everything figured out, and is ready to deliver the final blow that will save the day, wrap everything up, and allow him to go home. What he fails to take into account is that his own flaws have yet to be fully dealt with. They are blinding him to a crucial shortcoming in his plans, or causing him to misdirect his efforts.

As in Vera Caspary's classic murder mystery *Laura*. Homicide detective Mark McPherson isn't the only person to fall under beautiful socialite Laura's spell, but he's probably the first to have done so while she was dead. A case of mistaken identity returns her to the land of the living, and potentially to the arms of her treacherous fiancé. Battling a bad case of jealousy, at the 47.5% - 50% point, Mark plans to use Laura's unexpected reappearance to Trap the murderer into revealing himself. He tests it out on the maid with emotionally-shattering results, and then resets the scene for his prime suspect: the fiancé.

When the protagonist sets a Trap for the villain using himself as bait, it demonstrates the depth of his commitment to his goal. He's putting himself in the crosshairs, and if something goes wrong, he'll be the first to suffer. If the fate of someone else also hangs in the balance, then the stakes really skyrocket.

As in the television spy series *Burn Notice*, season three, episode two, entitled "Question and Answer." A divorced couple rely on burned CIA spy Michael Westen to recover their kidnapped son from ruthless extortioners engineering a diamond heist. Unable to get a lead on the boy's location, and with time running out, Michael implements a desperate and dangerous plan involving reverse interrogation. At the 47.5% - 50% mark, an undercover ally leads the villain to an isolated location where Michael, bound and helpless, awaits brutal questioning. Playing the role of bait, he plans to Trap the overconfident villain into revealing details about the child's location... provided he can avoid getting beaten to death in the process.

Proverbs 26:27 warns, "He that diggeth a pit shall fall therein." Sometimes the Trap the protagonist sets for the antagonist springs shut on himself, unravelling his own carefully-constructed internal defenses.

As in Merline Lovelace's RITA award-nominated romantic suspense *Stranded With a Spy*. Secret agent Cutter tracks down a disgraced political aide suspected of selling top secret banking secrets to hostile powers. Mallory's only ambition for her European getaway is escape from the sexual harassment scandal that ruined her life. By the 47.5% - 50% mark, Cutter's won his way into her confidence, and tries to Trap her into incriminating herself. Instead, her candid and fervent patriotism knocks the supports out from under his hard-earned cynicism, and he's left feeling like a heel.

STAKES CHARACTER

Sometimes it's the stakes character who's Trapped and helpless at the Midpoint. The stakes character is often the love interest, but can be any character emotionally connected to the protagonist. This is the person who will suffer the greatest should the protagonist fail and the villain succeed. The essence of the protagonist's hopes and fears are personified or wrapped up in this person. Thus the stakes character becomes the surrogate for a protagonist who doesn't put in a personal appearance or confrontation with the villain at the Midpoint.

As in the science fiction epic *Star Wars IV: A New Hope* (1977). A desperate holographic plea for help from Princess Leia (Carrie Fisher) ignites farm boy Luke's (Mark Hamill) quest to join the rebels and become a Jedi knight like his father. He joins Jedi master Obi-Wan (Alec Guinness) and smuggler Han Solo (Harrison Ford) on a mission to deliver the plans for the Empire's newest weapon to Leia's father for analysis. He's still in route to his destination at the 47.5% - 50% mark, but Leia is in the clutches of Darth Vader. Aboard the Death Star, Governor Tarkin condemns her to death. However, the threat of execution is not the real Trap. Tarkin presents her with an awful choice: betray the rebel base or watch her home planet blown to bits. Neither choice offers any hope of personal reprieve or escape. She is Trapped in a moral dilemma that will condemn innocents to die along with her, whatever she does.

When the power of the Trap is derived from an impossible moral dilemma, the story is tighter if that moral dilemma reflects and/or ups the stakes of a choice made earlier. Thereby, the writer uses the Midpoint to reassure readers everything that's happened so far is on point, and builds momentum toward a thematically meaningful resolution.

As in *Star Wars IV: A New Hope*. Early on, Luke was given the choice between joining the rebels (freedom) or staying home with his aunt and uncle (security). He rejected the rebels, and chose his family. At the time of his choice, the stakes seemed relatively low, but the Empire killed his family anyway. Now Leia is given a choice between betraying the rebels or saving her home planet. This time the stakes are vividly clear, with untold millions of lives in the balance. She *seems* to echo Luke's value choice when she betrays the rebels' base in favor of saving Alderaan. And again, the Empire kills innocent people anyway. Governor Tarkin mocks her trusting nature.

Making the same choice the same way twice with only higher stakes is insufficient to elevate the Midpoint to the dramatic power position it rightfully deserves. While reflective of an earlier moral dilemma, this time around something needs to be different. If both occasions involve the protagonist, that change indicates internal growth. Even if the Midpoint involves a surrogate, change is necessary to avoid predictability and, more importantly, highlight a new angle on the theme.

In *A New Hope*, Leia's betrayal of the rebels turns out to be a misdirection. She gave up an abandoned location, preserving not only the lives of the rebels actually within her power (she has no real power to save Alderaan), but also choosing the thematic value of freedom over security.

FURTHER READING

Suggestions to deepen your understanding of the Trap beat:

Christopher Vogler's *The Writer's Journey: Mythic Structure for Writers.* Chapter, "A Practical Guide." Chapter, "Stage Eight: The Ordeal." Available in print on Amazon and wherever books are sold.

Chihuahua Zero's online article, "5 Tips to Trap Your Characters." Currently available on The Write Practice at: http://thewritepractice.com/5-tips-to-trap-your-characters

"Quick Look"

Attack

Hallmark: *The antagonist launches a full-strength, take-no-prisoners assault against the protagonist.*

Use an Attack in the first half of your Midpoint to...

- Make things personal for the protagonist through the sacrificial death of a supporting character.
- Spur real internal growth when the protagonist is forced to change in order to survive.
- Demonstrate the protagonist's courage and commitment to his external goal or higher values in the face of overwhelming odds.
- Compel the protagonist's full commitment by burning the protagonist's bridges behind him, so the option to retreat or quit no longer exists.
- Show the cost of character growth when the protagonist's old support community turns against him as a "traitor" to the system.

(1st Half) Attack

The small glade at the Midpoint rings with a sudden explosion of violence. The protagonist desperately parries sword thrusts aimed not to wound or maim, but to kill. He stumbles on a vine and goes down.

The villain kicks the protagonist's only weapon out of reach and presses a sharp blade against his jugular. "You're going to die. Yes, and what you love most, too." He points to the helpless figure tied to a post sunk deep into the boggy ground, and the protagonist's heart clutches with agony.

Screenwriter and teacher Eric Edson in *The Story Solution* says at the Midpoint "conflict with the Adversary becomes personal," and a literal or metaphorical unmasking takes place. A literal or metaphorical death may even occur—either of a beloved character or the death of the protagonist's own self-delusions or defense mechanisms. (214)

Story consultant Christopher Vogler's reworking and simplification of mythologist Joseph Campbell's storytelling concept known as the Hero's Journey has made an indelible impact upon modern writers' understanding of story structure. In *The Writer's Journey: Mythic Structure for Writers, Second Edition*, Vogler says at every story's Midpoint, regardless of genre, "Heroes face death or something like it: their greatest fears, the failure of an enterprise, the end of a relationship, the death of an old personality..." (159) Obviously, if the hero really dies at the Midpoint and stays dead, the story would be pretty much over. Maybe the hero watches someone he cares about die, and is helpless to do anything about it. Maybe he finds himself responsible, either intentionally or unintentionally, for someone's demise. Death is an inescapably transforming event to endure, and all the more so when it has personal and emotional ramifications for the character.

Battling the protagonist's greatest fear requires triumphing over his own flawed nature. "The smoldering combat that ignites in the Ordeal may be an inner struggle between an old, comfortable, well-defended personality structure and a new one that is weak, unformed, but eager to be born." (Vogler 177)

The expansion of the protagonist's interests from himself to include others increases the stakes. The protagonist is no longer content merely looking out for Number One. He begins to hold himself accountable for the impact his behavior, both positive and negative, has on the wellbeing of others. In other words, the old selfish nature is attacked and killed at the Midpoint, and a new selfless nature is born. The second half of Act Two will then follow its struggle to grow, mature, and survive against mounting opposition.

The Attack is really about consequences. The protagonist has elbowed and pushed and charged ahead to reach his goal. He's stepped on some toes along the way. He's made mistakes, some acknowledged, but a few really important ones unacknowledged even to himself. They've unwittingly but inevitably placed him in a vulnerable position, exposed.

Now the consequences of his flawed behavior slap him right across the face. The antagonist attacks—not just to cut him off or trap him—but with the take-no-prisoners intention of annihilation. No more playing around, no more games. The antagonist intends for it to end here and now. To accomplish that, he ramps up the stakes by making his new attack painfully personal.

COLLATERAL DAMAGE

Often the Attack is where villains bring innocent supporting characters to die. This is a popular spot in mysteries for the murderer to strike again. Whereas the murder of a prime suspect Cuts Off the protagonist from pursuing a specific line of investigation and forces him to take a new direction, the murder of an innocent person who knows too much or just got too close is a personal Attack against the reader's and protagonist's sense of justice.

The villain may Attack innocent people simply to prove he *can.* He has the power and he demonstrates his willingness to use it. The fact that innocent people suffer or even die increases the intimidation factor and lets it be known this is total war. Nothing is off the table.

As in *Star Wars IV: A New Hope* (1977). Rebel forces threaten the evil Galactic Empire, who's just commissioned a new secret weapon called the Death Star. Governor Tarkin captures Princess Leia trying to send the weapon's blueprints to her father on Alderaan for analysis. At the 47.5% - 50% mark, he sentences her to death. She's defiant about her own demise, but when he compels her to choose between betraying the location of the rebels' base or watching her home planet blown to bits, she crumbles. As soon as he has the coordinates to the rebels' base, he orders the Death Star to fire on Alderaan anyway. "No star system will dare oppose the emperor now." She's forced to witness her entire home planet along with her family totally destroyed. That's pretty personal. But Tarkin twists the knife in deeper, Attacking her values and beliefs. "You're far too trusting." Now that's personal.

RUN TO THE ROAR

The protagonist may know well in advance that to cross the villain means inviting Attack and certain destruction, but the only way to reach his goal means facing hell head-on. This kind of awareness and foreknowledge tests and tempers the protagonist's resolve as he prepares for a classic Midpoint confrontation.

As in the classic film *The African Queen* (1951). At the outbreak of WWI German troops in Africa leave English missionary Rose (Katherine Hepburn) destitute and river steamboat captain Charlie (Humphrey Bogart) on the run. She presses him into joining her plan to sink an enemy warship that dominates a strategic waterway. But first they must navigate a wildly hostile river that passes right under a German fortress. Aware they have all the chances of fish in a barrel, Charlie basically gives himself up for dead. At the 47.5% - 50% mark, Charlie and Rose come in sight of the fearsome fortress and make their mad dash. The Germans open fire, peppering the boat with lead until it drifts helplessly beneath the onslaught. At first Charlie lays low and tries to wait it out, which has been his flawed response to life in general. But soon he realizes they won't survive that way. He has to change and be courageous, take the initiative. Charlie braves the hail of bullets to make stopgap repairs and get the boat moving again, but his desperate act literally places him in the crosshairs of a German sniper. The glare of the sun saves him at the last possible second, and they live to fight the enemy another day.

VALUES UNDER ASSAULT

Sometimes the antagonist admires the protagonist's unique abilities so greatly he wants the hero to switch sides and play on the antagonist's team. He needs the protagonist still standing, skills intact, but the protagonist's values system has got to go. So he tailors his Attack to utterly destroy the protagonist's moral defenses and compel unconditional surrender. This kind of Attack pressures the protagonist to change for the worse, therefore testing his belief in and commitment to specific core values. It is a common element of Midpoints involving series protagonists.

As in David Thompson's Wilderness Series western adventure *Comanche Moon.* Legendary frontiersman Nate King gets more than he bargains for when he rescues a greenhorn couple from bloodthirsty Comanches and a psychotic mountain man. The husband's stubborn foolhardiness nearly gets them killed and alienates his young wife. It isn't long before she's gazing at Nate with new eyes. At the 47.5% - 50% mark, Cynthia finds happily-married Nate alone on guard duty late at night and reveals her feelings for him. He fights to steer her affections back in her unwitting husband's direction. The dialogue scene bristles with martial terminology, leaving no mistake in the reader's awareness that this is an Attack of the most deeply personal nature. Can she conquer Nate's innermost values and defeat his devotion to his wife so as to permit an extramarital affair? He adroitly holds his own, until she discovers his blind spot—an unquenchable pride and passion for book-learning.

SUPPORT SYSTEM REVOLTS

The protagonist's old world and support system in Act One relied on his flaws to maintain the status quo. His experimenting with change, however unwillingly, in the first half of Act Two seriously disrupted a lot of lives. People may not be too happy to discover they can no longer automatically assume or depend upon his acting the same old dysfunctional way anymore. That includes the villain. The Attack may be the villain's determined effort to prevent the protagonist from growing or changing, and to reestablish by force the old status quo of Act One.

As in the cold war thriller movie *The Hunt for Red October* (1990). The USSR launches its newest submarine on its maiden voyage under the command of the Soviet navy's finest, Captain Marko Ramius (Sean Connery). When he ignores orders and heads for the United States, world powers tremble at the possible threat of either a rogue nuclear attack or high-level defection. Soviets and Americans scramble in a high-stakes race to find the sub first. Aware Ramius is making a high-stakes break for freedom, his own "side" is determined to kill him before he can successfully change his life and upset their status quo by delivering a military prize to the United States. At the 47.5% - 50% mark, the *Red October* is navigating a complicated maze of narrow underwater canyons when a Russian TU-95 Bear Aircraft spots the sub and immediately Attacks.

PROTAGONISTS NEED NOT APPLY

This is the only first-half Midpoint beat that has no version where the protagonist can take the lead. Glimpses, Cut Offs, and Traps may be initiated and driven by either the protagonist or antagonist, but an Attack at this point seems almost the exclusive territory of the antagonist/villain.

There's a very good reason protagonist-driven Attacks on this side of the Midpoint are rare. Readers derive meaning and significance in a story from the protagonist's internal growth and change. The first and second halves of the Midpoint are set up as stimulus and response to facilitate that change. Something happens in the Midpoint's first half that a character must respond to in the second half. Protagonists may learn from their own Glimpses, Cut Offs, or Traps, but Attacks are fully-committed attempts to wipe out the opposition, requiring the laser-focus of a mind closed to alternatives. The villain Attacks in the first half, forcing the protagonist to *change* in the second half in order to survive. If the protagonist Attacked in the first half, it would place the responsive burden of growth on another character, skewing the focus of the whole story. Readers might wonder if they were following the right character.

The protagonist may plan or even attempt to Attack the villain at the first-half Midpoint, but something gets in the way or otherwise prevents his going through with it. He erroneously believes he knows enough and is committed enough to end the villain's wrongdoing once and for all, right here, right now. For the protagonist to maintain reader empathy while considering such extreme action at this point, it's important the protagonist isn't the only one the villain has caused undue suffering. Innocents have been hurt, as well, and more will continue to be harmed if nothing is done. While the protagonist may be tempted by personal revenge, stopping the villain now is more about self-defense and protecting the innocent.

As in Lauran Paine's western *Open Range*. Boss Spearman and Charley Waite are freerangers minding their own business when they cross paths with tyrannical land baron Denton Baxter. When Baxter's threats turn into coldblooded murder, Boss and Charley decide to do unto others before anything more gets done to themselves or some other unsuspecting soul. At the 47.5% - 50% mark, Boss and Charley stalk the men posted guard over Boss's looted goods. But one thing after another interferes with their purpose. First, the men aren't all together in one place; some have been posted elsewhere. Then the discovery of Boss's hidden money box injects the tired men with renewed alertness. Finally, Boss and Charley discover the men in their sights are not the murderers they seek. Their planned Attack never comes off. Which is why I would more likely characterize an *attempted* Attack such as Boss and Charley's as a Cut Off, because their plans are Cut Off and they are forced to change direction.

FURTHER READING

Suggestions to deepen your understanding of the Attack beat:

Wendell Wellman's *The Writer's Roadmap*. Chapter 15, "The Midpoint Shift." Available in print on Amazon and wherever books are sold.

John Truby's *The Anatomy of Story: 22 Steps to Becoming a Master Storyteller*. Chapter 8, "Plot." Available in ebook and print on Amazon and wherever books are sold.

Mix and Match – Part 1

Kneeling at the base of the bomb, you rock back on your heels and examine your work. You've got your protagonist tied up in knots, but maybe there's a little extra length of fuse you'd like to utilize or some more story threads you'd like to tie into the central explosive tension. It's a good opportunity to add some more loops to the Midpoint bow.

Each of the four beats that may appear at the first-half Midpoint—Glimpse, Cut Off, Trap, and Attack—can stand alone or be creatively mixed and matched into pairs. If the story is lengthy or supports important subplots, then both beats may be given their own separate scenes at the Midpoint. More commonly the paired beats play off each other within a single event.

Focusing the first-half Midpoint event on only one or two kinds of beats, instead of squeezing in three or all four, preserves the dramatic balance between pacing and motivation. The Midpoint exerts pressure on the protagonist to grow and change. The need has become urgent. He can't put it off any longer. But his response, in order to be convincing and significant, has to carry the weight of proper deliberation and consideration. In other words, he has to be aware of what he's doing. The change he's making to his priorities and behavior must be intentional.

Confronting him with one or two different beats at the first-half Midpoint gives him a sufficient push in the right direction, while also allowing him time to own the action that must necessarily follow. Three or four kinds of beats might feel too chaotic or melodramatic, mutating a purposeful protagonist into a panicky one. In other words, avoid overkill. The protagonist doesn't need to Glimpse a possible resolution, *and* be Cut Off, *and* Trapped, *and* Attacked... all at the same Midpoint. He may be stubborn, but he's also smart enough to catch on from a couple carefully-chosen, well-developed beats.

What about an epic novel or movie with a large cast of characters and multiple story lines? Picking two or at most three different beats to echo and repeat in the various story threads can help tie them together, providing balance and resonance. (See the analysis of Herman Wouk's *Winds of War* in the "Additional Examples" chapter.)

Then there's the issue of space or real estate to consider. Remember, the first-half Midpoint event is only 2.5%. That's under ten pages in a 100,000 word novel. About two to three minutes in a full-length movie. A single minute in a modern television episode. These constraints necessarily condense, sharpen, and hone the Midpoint to needle-like precision and impact. Yet, as the examples below demonstrate, this is more than enough room to successfully explore a couple beats simultaneously.

CONFLICT

A classic implementation of Midpoint beats is where the protagonist and antagonist use them to advance their purposes while locked in conflict. This assures a Midpoint charged with energy and not driven by happenstance. The characters *make* it happen this way by the weapons they chose to wield against each other.

As in the classic wartime love story *Casablanca* (1942). The antagonist's attempt to inspire change in the protagonist by showing him a Glimpse of the truth is Cut Off by a Protagonist putting up his last desperate defense against additional pain. Nightclub owner Rick (Humphrey Bogart) famously "sticks his neck out for no one." Until *she* walks in—the woman who broke his heart—on the arm of a revered resistance leader fleeing the Nazi Gestapo. Suddenly his cynical facade starts falling apart, and he can't help himself from trying to find out what went wrong all those years ago. At the 47.5% - 50% mark, Ilsa (Ingrid Bergman) returns after hours to Rick's club and finds him alone with a bottle of booze. To win his help getting herself and her companion out of the country, she tries to explain what really happened before. She starts to provide a true Glimpse of the backstory. Because Rick still loves her, he can't hear her story without being moved. But cynicism is his shield, his flaw, and he's afraid of letting it go lest he be hurt again. So he ruthlessly Cuts Off her gentle explanations with insults that drive her away in tears.

Sometimes the antagonist is emboldened by his success at Cutting Off the protagonist's forward movement, and quickly moves in for the Attack. A stakes character emotionally connected to or otherwise integral to the achievement of the protagonist's goal may play surrogate for the hero here. While reasonably certain the main character will pull through the direst peril at this point, readers can't predict with equal confidence the survivability of favorite supporting characters. Tension will skyrocket with the sense that death or debilitating loss is a real possibility.

As in the autobiographical Vietnam war movie *We Were Soldiers* (2002). In the first major engagement between American soldiers and the North Vietnamese, Lt. Col. Hal Moore and 450 men find themselves dropped unexpectedly in the middle of 2,000 battle-hardened Communist forces. Outnumbered and surrounded, at the 47.5% - 50% mark, a US platoon is Cut Off from retreat or reinforcement. The enemy waits until the platoon's water gives out and their ammunition runs low, then launches a devastating Attack designed not only to utterly wipe out the platoon but also damage Lt. Col. Moore's will to fight.

If the protagonist gets wind of a Trap set and waiting for him by the antagonist, he may launch a counter plan to foil the antagonist's efforts. However, he discovers too late he possesses insufficient knowledge of the opposition arrayed against him, or of his own weaknesses. His plan is Cut Off, leaving him worse off than before.

As in Lauran Paine's western *Open Range*. When freerangers Boss and Charley run afoul of tyrannical land baron Denton Baxter, their companions are cruelly murdered or maimed, and everything they own is stolen. At the 47.5% - 50% mark, Baxter uses their possessions as bait to lure Boss and Charley into a deadly Trap. Tipped off by allies in town, Boss and Charley set out to get Baxter before he gets them. Their plan is Cut Off by one discovery after another of exactly how much they don't know, and they are compelled to literally change direction.

MOTIVATION

Sometimes a Glimpse triggers the protagonist to Cut Off the path he's on himself and change direction on his own initiative. Because this is the first-half Midpoint and his character growth is still incomplete, the change in direction initiated by the protagonist may be for the worse.

As in Debbie Macomber's contemporary romance *The Way to a Man's Heart*. Stuffy literature professor Grey has fallen in love with lively waitress Meghan. At the 47.5% - 50% mark, he Glimpses her across a school cafeteria chatting and laughing with new friends. Innocent enough, if he knew what was really going on. But he *falsely* perceives it as a harbinger of heartbreak to come. Sinking into despair that he's unable to change and become the type of man capable of holding her interest as well as her heart, he calls her up and without explanation Cuts Off their relationship.

Often the protagonist doesn't want to see the truth. The lies he's bought into provide a kind of perverted comfort or security. So he stays on the move so the truth won't catch up with him. Deep down he knows when it does, he won't have any option but to change. But the antagonist may have to Trap him to hold him still long enough to force him to Glimpse the truth.

As in T.L. Hines' paranormal thriller *The Dead Whisper On.* Candace is recruited by supernatural forces to "help" humanity. She's also warned to stay ahead of Keros, a powerful killing machine bent on stopping the beings she works with. After a violent battle, at the 47.5% - 50% mark, Candace wakes up Trapped by Keros on an airplane. Except instead of finishing her off, he gives her a true Glimpse of exactly who she's been working for.

ALLIES

An Attack may clear the way and prepare the stage for the protagonist to Glimpse a possible outcome or resolution for his hopes and dreams. This combination provides the one semi-exception to the "antagonists only" rule of thumb concerning Attacks at the first-half Midpoint. When the Attack enables the protagonist to personally experience a true Glimpse, often the Attack is carried out against the villain by allies of the protagonist in sympathy with his cause or goal. The protagonist still doesn't personally participate in the battle, though he may consult on timing, provide moral support, and/or coordinate mutual interests.

Also, the ally doing the Attacking has probably already reached the full measure of his own character growth.

As in the biographical movie *MacArthur* (1977). Tricked into quitting the Philippines in the face of overwhelming enemy assault, Gen. Douglas MacArthur (Gregory Peck) is driven to fulfill his promise to return. After twisting FDR's presidential arm, at the 47.5% - 50% mark, MacArthur steps onto the beaches of Leyte and announces triumphantly to the Philippine people, "I have returned." He urges the oppressed and beleaguered Filipinos to rise and Attack! As the resulting "line of battle rolls" across the island, MacArthur speeds to the front lines. "You can't fight the enemy if you can't see him!" There he receives news of his promotion to Commanding General of the Army and his fifth star. It's a Glimpse of a victorious future shining with possibility.

MAKE IT WORSE

The antagonist at the Midpoint doesn't just entrench his position. He gets aggressive and goes after more ground. If the story has a villain (a morally evil antagonist), he abandons whatever moral restraint might have held him in check and crosses a moral line previously assumed by the protagonist as safe or sacrosanct. If this manifests as a physical Attack, it can be made all the more personally painful to the protagonist and thematically significant to readers when it's presaged by a moral Trap. Capturing the protagonist in an impossible choice between two rights or two wrongs is a great way for the villain to manipulate the protagonist into a position of shared responsibility for the resulting Attack.

As in the science fiction space opera *Star Wars IV: A New Hope* (1977). Princess Leia is captured trying to deliver the schematics for the evil

Galactic Empire's new secret weapon to her father on Alderaan. At the 47.5% - 50% mark, Governor Tarkin condemns her to death for treason, and gives her a choice. Give him the location of the rebels' base, or watch the Death Star destroy Alderaan. She's Trapped in an impossible moral dilemma. If she saves her home planet, she condemns everyone to tyranny under the Galactic Empire. If she protects the rebels, she signs her family's death sentence. Either way, he's Trapped her into unwillingly cooperating with his Attack on one or the other group of innocent people. When she gives up a rebel location, Tarkin unleashes the Death Star's annihilating power against Alderaan anyway.

SUBPLOTS

Subplots have their own beginning, middle, and end. They have their own Midpoint, as well. A subplot's Midpoint can fall anywhere in Act Two, but usually it occurs fairly close to either side of the main story's Midpoint. Proximity may be determined by how influential the subplot is to the main story. If the subplot is largely independent of the main story until Act Three, then its Midpoint may occur at some distance from the central story's Midpoint. On the other hand, if the subplot is highly influential to the main story, braiding in and out at regular intervals, then its Midpoint may occur right on top of the main Midpoint in back-to-back scenes.

As in the Cold War tech thriller *The Hunt for Red October* (1990). Soviet submarine commander Marko Ramius captains the crown jewel of the Russian navy straight for the United States, in defiance of his orders. The west scrambles to cut him off, anticipating a nuclear assault. The communist east scrambles to catch him before he defects with their newest weaponry. At the 47.5% - 50% mark, there are two scenes. The first is the Midpoint in a subplot directly influencing the conflict in the main story. The American ambassador ruthlessly Traps the Soviet ambassador in a lie so lame it provides the Americans with exactly the political opening they need to arrive closer to the truth. The second scene is the first-half Midpoint in the main story, where a Soviet aircraft catches *Red October* in a maze of narrow undersea canyons and Attacks with torpedoes.

Second Half of the Midpoint

Mosquitoes buzz your ears, and you swat them away. Something big and long slithers unseen through the undergrowth beyond the glade's perimeter. The first half of the story securely tied to the Midpoint, you're ready to hike out of here.

But wait! Something on the ground at your feet catches your attention. It's the scarlet fuse leading to the second half of the story, waiting to be connected to the bomb. Now that you've made the first half of the bow, it's time to form the second half and twist them together into a tightly secured knot around the central tension point in the story.

After the stimulus has been given to the protagonist by either a Glimpse, Cut Off, Trap, or Attack beat at the first-half Midpoint, it's time for him to decide on an appropriate response. This is the domain of the second-half Midpoint, the event that also happens to launch the second half of the entire story.

Similar to the first half of the Midpoint, the second half performs **four** vital functions in the story:

- It delivers new information to the protagonist that demands a different response than before.
- It highlights conflicting thematic values and compels the protagonist to choose between them, reversing key roles.

- It combines higher stakes with increased urgency to push the protagonist past the point of no return.
- It forces the protagonist to get proactive and aggressive about what he *needs* internally, not just what he *wants* externally.

If the first half of the Midpoint has accomplished its job, the protagonist heads into the second half already convinced his flawed way of doing things not only won't work anymore, but that nothing short of death (professional, physical, or psychological) is on the line. Intellectual assent, however, is not enough to satisfy any reader. James 2:20 KJV says, "Faith without works is dead." The protagonist can neither rest on his laurels nor wallow in his misery. He must make a decision and take corresponding action based on his new convictions, or the story will die a disappointing and premature death.

How does the second-half Midpoint get the protagonist into gear for what lies ahead in the last half of the story? Similar to the first half, the second half also plays host to **four** beats that vividly translate its dramatic functions onto page and screen. Again, *all four don't show up in the same Midpoint, but at least one of them always does.* They can also be mixed and matched, as discussed in a later chapter.

In brief, the second-half Midpoint's four types of beats are:

- A character asks **Questions** and/or gets **Answers**.
- The protagonist must choose between **Love versus Goal.**
- A character **Escapes**.
- The protagonist **Attacks** the antagonist.

Some of these beats may seem to naturally follow others from the first-half Midpoint. For example, an Escape may seem the most logical and realistic response to being Trapped. But as the examples in the following chapters demonstrate, exciting and riveting Midpoints can be created from absolutely any combination. The most obvious response may indeed provide the perfect spark igniting the last half of the story, but keep an open mind about every option. Selecting which beats to twist together at the Midpoint depends primarily on the unique needs of the story and the external/internal journey of the characters.

Toss different protagonists into the same first-half Midpoint event, and each one will respond differently in the second half. Take a romantic suspense, for example, a genre that has to balance plot and character in more or less equal measure. Suppose at the first-half Midpoint, the bad guys Trap the hero and heroine, taking them prisoner.

If the hero is a shoot-first type, advancing both the plot and his character arc may require his slowing down for some Q & A concerning the best way to get out of this mess.

If the heroine is a brainy computer whiz, advancing both the plot and her character arc may require getting physical and Attacking her captors.

If one of them is seriously injured, advancing both the plot and either's character arc may require forcing them to choose between Love versus their Goal of stopping the bad guys.

Try another example, this time from a genre known for being "character-driven"—women's fiction. Instead of bad guys with guns, the heroine is dealing with something way more frightening. Teenagers with hormones. And the first-half Midpoint just gave her a terrifying Glimpse of her future. It looks like her husband's looking over the fence, her daughter's blowing off college to run away with an outlaw biker, and early-onset menopause will drive her into an untimely, unfulfilled grave.

If she's an aggressive, take-charge type who's flaw is dominating others, keeping the plot active while advancing her internal journey may require her to throw up her hands and try to Escape her troubles.

If she's an empathetic, nurturing type who's flaw is possessiveness, keeping the plot active while advancing her internal journey may require her to choose between Love versus Goal, and decide loving her family means setting them free.

If she's a quiet, easy-going type who's flaw is avoiding conflict at any cost, keeping the plot active while advancing her internal journey may require Attacking her problems head-on, such as ripping out the would-be home-wrecker's hair and confronting the biker boyfriend in his lair.

Of course, while the Midpoint takes a big step to advance the protagonist's character arc, the story isn't over. He still has old beliefs that must be knocked down in the next sequence, and another up or down moment awaits at the break into Act Three to test the resolve of his new convictions. Later in Act Three he will prove to himself and the reader whether or not he's truly learned and embraced the internal lessons that the external plot sought to teach him.

The following chapters describe each of the second-half Midpoint's four beats in greater detail, with multiple examples from many genres demonstrating a variety of interpretations. Set your imagination free as you explore them.

FURTHER READING

Suggestions to deepen your understanding of the Midpoint:

Darcy Pattison's online article, "Midpoint Crisis: Plotting." Currently available on Fiction Notes at: www.darcypattison.com/first-drafts/midpoint-crisis-plotting

Naomi L. Quenk's *Was That Really Me? How Everyday Stress Brings Out Our Hidden Personality.* The stress patterns of 16 personality types using Myers-Briggs Type Indicator. Available in ebook and print on Amazon and wherever books are sold.

"Quick Look"

Q & A

Hallmark: *The quest for or discovery of new information triggers a change in the protagonist's plans, behavior, or perspective.*

Use a Q&A in the second half of your Midpoint to...

- Plant essential clues to solving a mystery or conundrum.
- Demonstrate the protagonist's persistence, cleverness, and creativity in ferreting out the truth.
- Raise the stakes when the answers the protagonist gets hit too close to home, exposing previously unacknowledged emotions.
- Influence a character's intentions or decisions by revealing pertinent backstory information.
- Cast doubt or suspicion on alliances or motives.
- Explore the pros and cons of specific values associated with the story's theme.

Questions & Answers

Reeling from his encounter with the antagonist upon first stepping into the Midpoint clearing, the protagonist spies what looks like carvings covering a giant slab of rock. Clawing aside the mossy overgrowth with his bare hands until his fingers bleed, he uncovers a crude map identifying a few landmarks he remembers passing and pinpointing his present location.

Realization hits him like a blow. Those landmarks weren't friendly lighthouses as supposed, but enemy guard towers. Instead of nearing civilization, he's deep behind enemy lines in the Great Swampy Middle!

Writer and teacher Larry Brooks in his popular book, *Story Engineering,* emphasizes the importance of new information discovered or delivered at the Midpoint that changes the meaning of everything that's happened so far in the story. This change in context "activates new decisions, behaviors, and actions stemming from a new perspective." (192)

The Midpoint awakens the protagonist to the necessity to change, if he's going to achieve his goal. "The hero starts to conquer inner demons and begin doing things a little differently than before, or at least come to understand how they have been standing in his own way." (154) This kind of change can't happen on its own. A stimulus is required. "Something—new information, new awareness—needs to enter the story to serve as a catalyst for the hero's evolution." (154)

This new information Brooks champions as integral to a properly-constructed Midpoint is the second-half Midpoint beat called Questions & Answers. The key to this beat is the protagonist must desperately *want* to know the information. It has to be so vitally important to him, that when he finds out the truth, the import he's already placed on it motivates him to change in response. If the first half of the Midpoint did its job correctly, the urgent stimulus to ask certain Questions and get specific Answers has already been well established.

Because the information learned at the Question & Answers motivates the protagonist to make a significant change, the information is *always true*. Characters may lie at other times in the story, but not here. This is a meeting with hard truths that can no longer be ignored.

That doesn't mean the truth is easily won. It often has to be fought for, or a high price paid to demonstrate to readers the protagonist's commitment to facing the truth—whatever it might be. Investing something precious in gaining it makes it all the more valuable and influential.

This quest to get at the truth come hell or high water often necessitates getting it "straight from the horse's mouth." That most likely means braving or initiating a direct confrontation with the antagonist or villain. Of course, the antagonist/villain may be motivated just as strongly to withhold the answers the protagonist seeks. This is a favorite construct in mysteries, where often a death at the first-half Midpoint triggers the authorities to round up suspects for questioning in the second-half of the Midpoint.

Though the real murderer is highly motivated to obfuscate and conceal the truth of his own involvement, an important clue (possibly the most tell-tale clue of the whole mystery) will invariably be revealed. Almost just as invariably it's misunderstood, discounted, or discredited initially by authorities, but the clue catches the protagonist's attention as both true and significant. He just doesn't know yet how it fits into the puzzle or whom it points toward.

In mysteries, sometimes the authorities themselves act as unwitting surrogates for the murderer by insisting on filtering new information through previously established assumptions the villain has helped create. The protagonist may struggle to wrestle important information from close-minded or corrupt authorities about autopsies, DNA, fingerprints, time of death, alibis, etc., only to have their interest disdained for challenging accepted theories. "We already know who did it. Quit wasting our time with all these questions."

Mysteries or suspense may put a twist on the Question & Answer beat by having the authorities round up the protagonist and question him as the prime suspect. Again, the authorities have been prejudiced by the villain and unknowingly act as his instruments in this confrontation. In this case, the new information the protagonist discovers is not found in the answers he himself gives, but in the intent behind the questions asked. He finds out he's being set up, framed, and the real murderer is taking action to eliminate the protagonist from the equation. Gaps or holes in his own knowledge, previously considered harmless, may suddenly take on threatening significance and ramifications.

THE TRUTH IS TRICKY

In suspense stories, where the villain is a known threat instead of a puzzle to be solved, the protagonist may have to get creative about gaining the truth. He needs to know specific data about the villain's plans, strength, resources, victims, and/or henchmen. The villain doesn't want to give up this information, because information is power. What the protagonist doesn't know, *can* be used to hurt him or other innocent people. The villain knows this, and more than likely is playing it close to the vest. So the protagonist may have to infiltrate the enemy's camp, assume a false identity, or feign powerlessness to gain the villain's confidence or throw him off guard and trick him into letting something slip.

As in the third season episode of the television spy series *Burn Notice*, "Questions and Answers." Michael helps a divorced couple try to rescue their son from ruthless kidnappers plotting a diamond heist. In the first half of the Midpoint, he sets a Trap for the criminal mastermind by pretending to be a junkie with information about the kidnapping. The villain is motivated to find out who on his team has been leaking his plans, and intends to beat the truth out of the helpless "junkie." At the 50% - 52.5% mark, Michael's risky and carefully choreographed plan goes into action as the brutal interrogation begins. His every answer is skillfully crafted to glean information about the boy's whereabouts from the villain's questions.

LET'S TALK ABOUT LOVE

Of course, the Questions & Answers beat isn't limited to mysteries or suspense. It's effective at raising the stakes and providing direction in romances, too. Some of the most enduring questions in human history are about love, such as the timeless inquiry, "How do you know when you're in love?"

As in Debbie Macomber's contemporary romance *Rainy Day Kisses*. All-business-no-play Susannah bonds with her hunky neighbor while babysitting her fussy infant niece. In the first half of the Midpoint, she experiments with letting her hair down and simply relaxing for a change. Flying kites with Nate in the park gives her a beguiling Glimpse of a possible future with him. After the date, at the 50% - 52.5% mark, she hunts down her sister (an accomplished housewife) to quiz her for girly info that's suddenly taken on vital importance to career-driven Susannah. How do you know a man is The One? (A: His kiss.) How do you catch him? (A: His favorite food.) And how do you make chocolate chip cookies without setting off the smoke alarm? (A: Remove the batteries.)

Sometimes all a broken heart wants to know is what went wrong. If the Big Breakup happened at the first-half Midpoint, it's virtually guaranteed the rejected party is going to want answers. The second-half Midpoint is where he or she will come looking for them.

As in Debbie Macomber's contemporary romance *The Way to a Man's Heart*. Literature professor Grey ignites waitress Meghan's latent hopes and dreams, not only for a higher education, but for love. She knows they have a special connection. That's why when he abruptly Cuts Off their relationship at the first-half Midpoint, she's hurt and blindsided. At the 50% - 52.5% mark, she gathers her courage and shows up unannounced at his office to find out why he broke up with her. Shielding his own insecurities behind an aloof facade, he resists answering her questions until at last he sends her in humiliated retreat from his office.

The path of love may not only be rocky, it may be blocked by a giant boulder. A romantic rival. There's a reason all's fair in love and war. Not only are the stakes high, but a lot of tactics involved are the same. An essential rule of war (and love) is "know your enemy." Since love triangles are a classic personification of thematic conflicts tugging at the protagonist, "know your enemy" is a mirror of "know yourself." Before the protagonist can ask the right questions, he must be brutally honest with himself about what kind of answers he's after.

As in James Oliver Curwood's bestselling historical romance *The Flaming Forest.* RCMP David Carrigan is hot on the trail of a vicious murderer when he's taken captive by the beautiful Marie-Anne. Convinced the murderer is somehow connected with the legendary riverman St. Pierre—perhaps even one and the same—David is stunned when Marie-Anne claims to be St. Pierre's wife. David's inner turmoil reaches new heights at the first-half Midpoint when a brief embrace provides a Glimpse into his own heart and the deep love he harbors for her. At the 50% - 52.5% mark, the long-awaited St. Pierre returns. David watches the couple's joyous reunion, seeking answers about the discordant mating of a delicate wildflower with a monster. Then he realizes his jealousy is distorting the truth. His rival is no monster, but a mighty, beloved chief to the river people…and to Marie-Anne.

BACKSTORY

Revealing a character's backstory at the Midpoint is an effective way to raise the stakes and validate deeply rooted internal flaws and conflicts. If unveiled at the first-half Midpoint, backstory appears as a Glimpse often expressed as a freewill token of trust in a relationship. If held in reserve until the second-half Midpoint, revealing the backstory is focused on setting the record straight and correcting flawed assumptions ruling other characters' actions and reactions. Honestly answering long-simmering questions puts an implicit demand on the other person to respond differently now that the truth is known.

As in James Oliver Curwood's historical romance *The Hunted Woman.* A reclusive writer defends a mysterious woman from human traffickers while helping her search for her husband's grave in the mountains of Alaska. Discovering the burial site at the first-half Midpoint, she demands proof it actually belongs to her husband. The hero assumes her obsession is fueled by a deathless love for the man she lost, thus rendering his own chances of winning her futile. At the 50% - 52.5% mark, she deliberately evokes his curiosity, volunteering bitter truths about her past and the predator who held her captive in a hated marriage. "I'm free!" she exults, igniting the hero's hope and determination to make her his own.

SCOUTING THE OPPOSITION

Sometimes answers obtained in the second-half Midpoint spawn even more urgent questions about alliances and motivations. The protagonist may seem to have his goal suddenly in hand only to discover, like the Trojans of old, he needs to investigate this gift horse more closely.

As in James Oliver Curwood's historical romance, *The Alaskan*. Alaskan rancher Alan falls in love aboard ship with beautiful and mysterious runaway Mary. When she's reported gone overboard, his desperate search for her body leads to feverish deliriums haunted by her ghost. At the first-half Midpoint, he arrives at his ranch and discovers his dreams have miraculously come true. Mary is alive, well, and waiting for him. But at the 50% - 52.5% mark, his queries into her hazardous journey quickly bring him back down to earth. New questions loom large concerning her motives and unexplained connection with his sworn enemy. Something compelled her to brave hell and high water to reach him, but whether it's love or treachery he can't be sure.

If the protagonist's plan fell apart in the first-half Midpoint, he needs fresh intelligence about his enemy's strengths. How could he fail so disastrously, when he thought he had all his bases covered? What did he miss? Even if the information comes too late to rescue victory from the jaws of defeat, it might mean the difference between giving up or surviving to fight another day.

As in Robert A. Heinlein's science fiction classic *The Puppet Masters.* Government agent Sam finds himself on the front lines of a war against invading aliens known as Masters. Mere hours ahead of a massive military clean-up of alien hotspots, he discovers at the first-half Midpoint that major cities in the United States have been surreptitiously saturated with Masters. At the 50% - 52.5% mark, as the country reels from losing the majority of its military in the disastrous Attack, questions fly thick and fast. Sam visits a laboratory for answers about the aliens' astonishingly rapid replication, and reassesses the enemy's prodigious strength. The truth is Sam and the remaining survivors are way worse off than previously believed.

THEME

Questions & Answers may concern issues of theme and whether or not changing is really worth the effort. The protagonist may feel discouraged and wonder if he's wise to take the leap of faith in his character growth.

As in the science fiction epic *Star Wars IV: A New Hope* (1977). Luke (Mark Hamill) has apprenticed himself under Jedi master Obi Wan Kenobi (Alec Guinness) to become a Jedi knight like his father. By the 50% - 52.5% mark, his training is progressing with disheartening slowness. His friend Han Solo (Harrison Ford) questions the value of believing in anything you can't see, while Obi Wan counsels patience and persistence. At last Luke experiences a fleeting success training with the Force, and Obi Wan announces, "You've taken your first step into a larger world."

FURTHER READING

Suggestions to deepen your understanding of the Questions & Answers beat:

Larry Brooks' *Story Engineering.* Chapter 24, "The Third Box: Part 3—The Attack." Chapter 34, "Wrapping Your Head Around the Mid-point." Available in ebook and print on Amazon and wherever books are sold.

Larry Brooks' online article, "*Shutter Island* — The Part 2 Pinch Point and the Mid-Point." Currently available on his blog, StoryFix, at: http://storyfix.com/7b-"shutter-island"---the-part-2-pinch-point-and-the-mid-point

Margo Lerwill's online article, "Story Structure Part 4 — The Mid-Point Twist." Currently available on her blog, Urban Psychopomp: http://urbanpsychopomp.blogspot.com/2011/05/story-structure-part-4-mid-point-twist.html

"Quick Look"

Love vs. Goal

Hallmark: *Conflicting loyalties challenge the protagonist to decide between his goal and an important relationship.*

Use Love vs Goal in the second half of your Midpoint to...

- Add a ticking clock.
- Sharpen conflict by committing the protagonist to a relationship at odds with his goal. (Often expressed as the "big love scene.")
- Make the protagonist desperately want something he believes he has no chance of winning.
- Advance the protagonist's internal growth from selfishness toward selflessness by establishing his commitment to someone else's cause without guarantee of benefit, reward, or reciprocity.
- Compel the protagonist to publicly acknowledge a long-denied loyalty.

Love vs. Goal

Grabbing his loved one's hand, the protagonist dashes toward the path leading out of the Midpoint glade. As he draws closer, he realizes the path forks. To his relief, the branch on the left is clearly marked: "External Want—this way."

Then his loved one's fingers slip apart from his and she plunges confidently down the opposite branch marked: "Internal Need—danger ahead."

He hesitates, but only for an instant, as the urgent moment of decision sinks in. Is he willing to give up what he thinks he wants for what he truly needs?

Emotional commitment plays an important role in changing the protagonist's way of doing things from this point on. The change in direction is reflected by a change in stakes. In the first half of the story, the protagonist primarily risks winning or losing something physical. At the same time, this external goal is self-focused. It's mostly about benefitting himself.

Thus the classic example of two starving dogs fighting over the same bone. Both want it. Both refuse to allow the other to have it.

Then, because of the Midpoint, the nature of the protagonist's hopes and fears undergoes an eyeopening change. While external conflicts and obstacles continue to buffet him in the second half of Act Two, the primary stakes are now personalized and internal. They also become other-focused. Now it becomes about someone else.

An event occurs that makes one of the dogs realize there's something else he needs worse than the bone. But he'll have to give up the bone to get it. Maybe a child who befriended him earlier cries for help. Will he lay aside his own desires to respond to someone else's situation?

Late writing guru Blake Snyder in *Save the Cat Strikes Back!* points out the urgency of the Midpoint relating to the protagonist's decision to grow and change. "'Stakes raised,' 'time clocks' forcing his decision, the hero must decide. What's it gonna be, pal: butterfly or worm? The Midpoint is where the hero stands up and says: Yes, I'm going through with this." (52)

The transformation Snyder suggested occurs here is why the Midpoint is where key character roles reverse or turn upside-down. Opponents become lovers, as in the romantic comedy *While You Were Sleeping.* Or a timid hobbit rises to become chief of a band of fierce dwarves and leads them on an adventurous quest, as in J.R.R. Tolkien's *The Hobbit.*

Writer and teacher John Vorhaus in *The Comic Toolbox* calls the Midpoint the place in the story when "the monkey wrench is thrown. A screw-up happens, a new threat arises, a new character enters, or a complication develops." Which might sound a little like throwing everything plus the kitchen sink at the protagonist. But Vorhaus digs deeper. "The new bad thing that happens is a change in the hero's state of mind." (87)

What makes the screw-up, new threat, new character, or complication that develops at the Midpoint different from other screw-ups, threats, characters, or complications elsewhere in the story? This time it *changes the hero's focus* from his goal to his need—from what he thinks will solve his problem to what he's willing to give up in order to satisfy a deeper longing.

What kind of Midpoint can make the stakes so highly personal for the protagonist that it changes his behavior? "The monkey wrench is usually thrown when the hero falls in love. Why is this a bad thing? Because it creates a dynamic and irreconcilable conflict between the character's original, self-serving goal and his new goal of winning his loved one's heart." (Vorhaus 88)

Love is the bedrock every positive thematic value is rooted in. Trust and fidelity work because of love. Hope and confidence are unashamed because of love. It is the only power strong enough to challenge and defeat the protagonist's greatest fear and redeem his fatal flaw from self-destruction.

Vorhaus's insight is equally applicable to romances and non-romances alike, because a protagonist's internal growth is most often externalized in a significant relationship. It may be romantic in nature. It may be platonic. It may be fraternal, parental, etc. It could be between a boy and his dog. What matters is that the protagonist cares about someone outside himself, and that relationship creates the stakes competing with his goal.

"The key word is 'loyalty,'" Vorhaus explains. "A character always starts out with loyalty to himself and loyalty to his goal. What happens when the money wrench is thrown is that the hero experiences *displaced loyalty*... Make him want two things and make it so that he can't have both."(88)

It's Love vs. Goal.

Which character is best designed to shift the protagonist's loyalty? The character who is his thematic opposite—the antagonist!

Script consultant and writing teacher Billy Mernit in *Writing the Romantic Comedy* defines the Midpoint as "a situation that irrevocably binds the protagonist with the antagonist (often while tweaking sexual tensions) and has further implications for the outcome of the relationship... It specifically speaks to the level of emotional involvement." (113-114) In romances, the love interest serves the dramatic role of antagonist. Aside from the comment about sexual tension, his definition could equally apply to any genre.

URGENCY

Love vs. Goal focuses on impressing upon the protagonist the inescapable reality of his displaced loyalty along with the inherent and irreconcilable conflict between the two things he now cares desperately about. He knows he'll have to choose between them sooner or later, but he probably wishes it was later instead of sooner. Of course, events in the plot and/or the antagonist won't allow him to put it off for long.

As in Debbie Macomber's contemporary romance *Rainy Day Kisses.* At the first-half Midpoint, career-driven Susannah lets down her hair and relishes a date with her hunky neighbor, Nate, who elevates relaxation to an art form. At the 50% - 52.5% mark, she appeals to her sister for relationship advice and comes to the uncomfortable conclusion she's falling in love. It couldn't happen at a worse time. The promotion she's worked so hard for is about to be announced, and she knows instinctively her carefully-planned life path will take a sharp turn off course if she becomes seriously involved with someone like Nate.

THE BIG LOVE SCENE

The Midpoint is a classic location for the Big Love Scene in romances. If it happens in the first half of the Midpoint, it contributes to the protagonist's motivation to change by providing a Glimpse of a possible outcome to the story. But if reserved for the second-half Midpoint, it wakes the protagonist up to the inherent conflict built into the relationship and his own displaced loyalty. The mutual intimacy shared between characters in a love scene means it's too late to think about putting off a choice between two wants. Ready or not, the protagonist is already committed to a course at cross-purposes with his goal.

As in Merline Lovelace's contemporary romantic suspense *Stranded With a Spy*. The closer that government spy Cutter gets to suspected traitor Mallory, the less convinced he becomes of her guilt. At the first-half Midpoint, his attempts to Trap her into incriminating herself backfire, leaving him feeling like a heel. At the 50% - 52.5% mark, he muzzles his conscience and gives in to their sizzling mutual attraction. But making love to Mallory seriously undermines his mission goal and causes him to betray his cover. It's too late to repair the damage or to turn away from his desire for the woman at the center of an international terrorist plot.

Sometimes the protagonist recognizes the higher value represented by the relationship and eagerly embraces the choice presented by the Love vs. Goal. However, he dug a very deep hole for himself pursuing his misguided goal in the first half of the story. Climbing free of it isn't going to be easy.

As in the romantic comedy *While You Were Sleeping* (1995). Lucy's long-cherished fantasy of marrying Peter comes close to reality when an accident lands him in a coma and she's mistaken by his family as his fiancee. She has her work cut out for her convincing his suspicious brother, Jack, the engagement is real. At the first-half Midpoint, a romantic stroll with Jack gives Lucy a Glimpse of a genuine relationship with someone she can laugh and grow old with. At the 50% - 52.5% mark, a series of slips on an icy sidewalk results in a clumsy, breathless embrace before parting at her door. It's a sweet, funny, kiss-less love scene. From that moment on, Lucy knows Jack—not his brother—is her real prince. Her landlord's son, Joe Jr., catches her in the hallway and confronts her with a choice. "All right, Lucy, it's either me or him." Without a moment's hesitation, she happily replies, "Him!"

In a way, Joe Jr. is to Lucy what Lucy is to Peter. He's delusional about their relationship, going so far as convincing other people they're intimately involved. He represents an extreme, albeit humorously harmless, version of Lucy herself. So when Joe Jr. demands she choose between "me and him," thematically she's choosing between her old self and new self. Her old set of values and behaviors versus a new set of values and behaviors. But she's done too good a job convincing everyone she's the fiancee. Her misguided goal suddenly becomes a bear trap holding her back from the very happiness she once believed it could provide. Jack will never betray his brother, and unless she can pull the plug on the fake relationship she once wanted, she'll never gain the real relationship she desperately needs in order to be truly happy.

LOVING THE ENEMY

The relationship at the focal point of the Love vs. Goal beat may not even seem attainable to the protagonist, but his displaced loyalty—and the conflict that comes along with it—is still real to him. More so than the possibility of winning her heart, it's the fact that he *values* the loved one as much or more than his misguided goal that creates the change in his state of mind.

As in James Oliver Curwood's historical romance *The Flaming Forest.* Close on the trail of a notorious murderer, RMCP David Carrigan falls in love with a woman he believes is the wife of his prime suspect. The first-half Midpoint gives him a Glimpse of how deep his feelings are for her. Then at the 50% - 52.5% mark, her "husband" returns. David witnesses their happy reunion, and realizes his love is hopelessly unrequited. Although he recognizes he has no chance to win Marie-Anne's heart away from so imposing a rival, his loyalty to her (and by extension to her values) is powerful enough to create conflict with his devotion to duty.

No man is an island, and nether is the protagonist. His goal is usually tangled up with other characters, such as allies, enemies, friends, family, stakes characters, and particularly the antagonist. Remember "antagonist" doesn't necessarily refer to a morally-evil villain, but simply means the character most strongly and personally opposed to the protagonist's goals.

Sometimes it's the antagonist who leads the way at the Midpoint by displacing loyalty to another person or cause threatening the protagonist's goals. The protagonist is then faced with the unavoidable choice of supporting the antagonist's new loyalties and by extension risk losing everything he's worked for, or cling to his old way of doing things and alienate an important relationship.

As in the comedy-drama *Steel Magnolias* (1989). M'Lynn's (Sally Fields) role as caring mother to a severely diabetic daughter (Julia Roberts) doesn't end when she sees her off to a new life as a married woman. At the first-half Midpoint, Shelby returns at Christmas to announce she's having a baby. The pregnancy is a high stakes gamble she's willing to take, even while M'Lynn rages at being Cut Off from say-so in her daughter's life. At the 50% - 52.5% mark, Shelby's already displaced her own loyalty from self-preservation to the life of her child. "I'd rather have thirty minutes of wonderful, than a lifetime of nothing special." She pleads with her mother to support her decision, but it's a hard transition for M'Lynn to consider when it might mean losing the daughter she's spent a lifetime loving and protecting.

CATCHING UP WITH THE TIMES

Sometimes the protagonist's loyalties were displaced earlier in the first half of the story, but he's avoided facing up to them. His behavior is already changing, but he clings to old rationalizations to avoid commitment. The Midpoint is also known as the Point of No Return for a good reason. It's where the protagonist commits to a new path, intentionally binding himself to a new course of action from which there can be no retreat. It's where avoidance and rationalizations die a permanent death.

As in the romantic comedy *People Will Talk* (1951). Dr. Noah Praetorius's unusual interest in a female suicide patient piques the awareness of his friends that something is different, but Noah insists his extraordinary involvement is purely professional. Even when he pursues Deborah weeks later into the country, he convinces himself it's for a purely humanitarian purpose. However, at the first-half Midpoint his "humanitarian" goal is gently but unequivocally Cut Off at the pass. At the 50% - 52.5% mark, Deborah turns the tables on him by confronting him with his real reason for finding her. He has the choice of telling her the pregnancy test was accurate after all (the original reason she tried to kill herself), or admitting he's in love with her. It's a clear case of Love vs. Goal. He chooses love and a speedy elopement.

FURTHER READING

Suggestions to deepen your understanding of the Love vs. Goal beat:

John Vorhaus's *The Comic Toolbox: How to Be Funny Even If You're Not.* Chapter 7, "The Comic Througline." Available in print on Amazon and wherever books are sold.

Viki King's *How to Write a Movie in 21 Days: The Inner Movie Method.* Chapter, "Your Random Draft; Write from Your Heart." Available in print on Amazon and wherever books are sold.

Rob Tobin's *The Screenwriting Formula: How It Works and How to Use It.* Chapter 12, "Act Two, Part Two." Available in print on Amazon and wherever books are sold.

Lydia Sharp's online article, "Writing Toward Your Midpoint." Currently available on The Sharp Angle at: http://lydiasharp.blogspot.com/2012/03/writing-toward-your-midpoint.html

"Quick Look"

Escape

Hallmark: *The protagonist tries to break free from the antagonist's confinement or control. Or, the antagonist tries to elude the protagonist.*

Use an Escape in the second half of your Midpoint to...

- Raise the stakes and increase urgency.
- Sustain story logic and credibility.
- Advance the protagonist's internal growth by compelling him to sacrifice a cherished symbol of his flaw.
- Set up an unguarded moment exposing latent emotions or desires.
- Demonstrate how the protagonist's own flaw sabotages his supposedly foolproof plan.
- Personalize larger stakes on an intimate level by rescuing a valued ally or surrogate character.

Escape

The protagonist unravels the last of the bonds fastening him to a cyprus tree like a sacrificial offering. A spear whistles through the air, and he ducks just in time as the heavy iron point splinters a deep wound in the wood where his head was a second ago. Dashing across the Midpoint glade, he senses the villain closing in behind him. Hot breath scalds the back of his neck. He scrapes together a burst of speed, straining every muscle to reach the path heading to the second half of the story.

Escapes can be about the protagonist fleeing or avoiding the antagonist/villain, or the antagonist/villain eluding the protagonist. Either way, this is not the last time the two will cross physical or psychological swords. While the protagonist may draw blood at the Midpoint, from a dramatic perspective he still requires the continued opposition of the villain in order to complete his character arc. Therefore, it's essential that if the big bad guy bites the dust at the Midpoint, it turns out he was only working for a bigger, badder guy who's the one really responsible for applying pressure to the protagonist. At the Midpoint, the true villain always lives to fight another day.

Often the protagonist will only pass the Point of No Return (aka Midpoint) because he's fleeing something dangerous, undesirable, or at a bare minimum unpleasant. In *The Writer's Journey, Second Edition* Christopher Vogler says, "Transformation is often an important aspect of chases and escapes." (197) The significance of any Midpoint beat is found not in the flashy trappings of plot alone, but in how plot influences the character's internal arc and growth. This is no less true of the Escape beat. No matter how physical or tangible the Escape is depicted, its true resonance within the story is the psychological drama of a character escaping the personification of inner demons and being forced to change his behavior in order to survive. (197)

Escape by definition naturally involves a person fleeing and another person who is chasing, trapping, or attacking. There will be dire consequences if the first person is caught or fails to get away from the second person. There's also usually a small window of time in which to make good the escape. Either the second person is closing in fast, or the trap is tightening to an unbearable level, or the first person can't hold out under a prolonged attack.

Stakes and urgency.

Late writer and teacher Blake Snyder boiled the Midpoint down to these two vital components necessary to make a story work: "the stakes are raised," and a "time clock" appears. In his online article "Midpoint—The Key to Cracking Any Story," he treats these two beats as a matched set that together are truly more than the sum of their parts. Combining stakes and urgency together at the Midpoint multiplies the dramatic power of both. The focal character cannot ignore stakes that are both unavoidable *and* urgent. To change the imminent consequences of success or failure, he must change something causing those consequences. The only thing truly within a character's power to change is his own attitudes, beliefs, and behaviors. Therefore, to change the inevitable outcome, he must change something within himself.

SYMBOLS

Internal change may be externalized as the protagonist's giving up something precious or valuable in order to secure their Escape. It may or may not seem valuable in the world's eyes, but it is worth much to the character who's compelled to sacrifice it. This works by turning the object in the first half of the story into a symbol of the character's flawed attitudes, beliefs, or behaviors. The symbolic relevance of the object doesn't have to be deep or mystical. In fact, it's better if it's simple and easily understood so the dramatic impact of its sacrifice is instinctively and instantaneously recognized. The reader should not have to pause and ponder a long time to figure it out. However, "simple" and "understood" is not a license for heavy-handedly beating the reader over the head with the obvious, "This is what the symbol means!" That robs all the fun out of the reader's discovering for themselves the dovetailing of plot and character. It's sufficient to set up the object as a symbol, then sit back and allow the reader to put two and two together.

It's a three-stage process. Here's how it works.

First, establish the object (sometimes it may be a physical gesture) early on via its value to a character. For example, in the comedy-adventure *Five Weeks in a Balloon* (1962), a prickly British officer insists on packing a fine porcelain tea set with him on a hazardous journey.

Second, associate a belief or emotion with the object. Bonus points if this belief or emotion is in conflict with another character's beliefs or emotions. For example, the Britisher never misses high tea, regardless of circumstances, because to him it's carrying on the spirit of the Empire. This irks his independent-minded Scottish navigator.

Third, show the symbol used in a new or different way that demonstrates a change in those beliefs or emotions. For example, when the Scottish navigator is taken captive by hostile Muslims bent on sacrificing him to the moon god, the Britisher deliberately smashes his precious teapot during a desperate rescue attempt. The audience understands, without being told, that the Britisher has come to value the Scotsman's friendship more than his own national pride.

Of course, symbols can show up anywhere in a story, not just at the Midpoint. But they take on special significance and carry greater meaning when utilized at key turning points in the story, such as act breaks, the Midpoint, and especially the final Climax (where they are virtually essential). So if the protagonist sacrifices a symbol at the Midpoint, make sure it's a stepping stone to greater change and not the end destination. Either he has a chance later on at the Climax of unexpectedly redeeming the symbol and chooses instead to let it go for good, *or* releases the real thing the symbol represented, *or* sacrifices a bigger/more valuable symbol of a bigger/root flaw.

UNAVOIDABLE

The Escape is often (but not always) the protagonist's logical and necessary response to a first-half Midpoint's Trap or Attack by the antagonist/villain. Tension is heightened in direct proportion to how hopeless the situation appears.

As in Suzanne Collins' dystopian fantasy *The Hunger Games*. At the first-half Midpoint, a gang of murderous tributes Trap Katniss up a tree, waiting only for daylight to finish her off. Tiny Rue proves an unexpected ally by covertly signaling to Katniss from a neighboring tree. Her one chance to maybe come out of this alive is to saw down a deadly tracker-jacker nest onto her enemies, without getting stung to death herself. At the 50% - 52.5% mark, dawn arrives and Katniss manages to successfully cut down the nest on top of the tributes, but is stung so badly she nearly passes out before she can Escape.

Sometimes the protagonist knows the antagonist/villain has set a Trap, and responds by boldly striding right into it. Either he erroneously disdains the villain's power to pull it off, or egotistically assumes he can outwit his enemy. Perhaps he's done it so many times before he mistakenly believes this time will be no different. It's a case of pride going before destruction. He doesn't realize yet that the villain hasn't been sitting around twiddling his thumbs, but has developed new powers or insight into the protagonist's vulnerabilities. He may have caught on to the protagonist's newly displaced loyalties, and leverages that knowledge to bait the trap with something irresistible.

As in the swashbuckler *The Adventures of Robin Hood* (1938). At the first-half Midpoint, evil Prince John and his minions plot to Trap the noble outlaw by hosting a prestigious archery tournament where Maid Marian will personally bestow the prize. At the 50% - 52.5% mark, Robin Hood shrugs off the concerns of his merry men (who warn him it's a blatant Trap). He delights at the prospect of outsmarting Prince John again, and can't resist a chance at seeing Maid Marian. His newly awakened love for her makes him deaf to wise counsel and risk his external goal of fighting for the oppressed in the absence of King Richard.

It may not be pride or love leading the protagonist to risk destruction, but rather sheer necessity. If the antagonist/villain stands directly between the protagonist and his goal, there may be no other way forward but full steam ahead. When the Midpoint plays out this straightforwardly, the element of surprise originates from within. The release of tension generated by a successful Escape from death can trigger a corresponding release of inhibitions and expose latent emotions and desires.

As in the classic adventure *The African Queen* (1951). At the outset of WWI, missionary Rose (Katherine Hepburn) and river captain Charlie (Humphrey Bogart) travel down a treacherous river to attack a German warship. At first their relationship is like soda and vinegar. At the first-half Midpoint, they steer the *Queen* directly beneath an enemy fortress's blazing guns, inviting a devastating Attack in their determination to reach their goal. At the 50% - 52.5% mark, they Escape both the German Attack and killer rapids. Their exuberant celebration at Escaping certain death results in a spontaneous embrace and kiss revealing newly displaced loyalties and sparking an unforeseen conflict that raises the stakes. Risking their own lives for a patriotic cause is one thing, but risking each other's life now that their hearts are involved is something quite different and colors their emotional conflict for the remainder of the story.

STAKES

Antagonists or villains may take the opportunity of the second-half Midpoint to warn the protagonist against Escaping, or to impress upon him the increased stakes of making an attempt. When all avenues of Escape seem blocked, but the protagonist refuses to give up, cave in, or quit, he proves his worthiness as someone to root for.

As in the romantic wartime drama *Casablanca* (1942). Ilsa (Ingrid Bergman) and her companion Victor Lazlo (Paul Henreid), a renowned freedom fighter, are trapped in Casablanca while fleeing the Nazis. Their best chance at salvation are some missing transit papers in the possession of Ilsa's jilted lover, Rick (Humphrey Bogart). At the first-half Midpoint, Ilsa's attempt to gain his help by explaining her side of their breakup is cynically Cut Off by a drunken Rick. Then at the 50% - 52.5% mark, German Major Strasser makes it plain to Ilsa and Lazlo exactly why any attempt to Escape from Casablanca would not only prove futile, but suicidal. Every possible exit has been sealed off to them, save the one that relies solely upon Rick completing his internal arc from cynicism to idealism.

Notice Rick appears in the first-half Midpoint, but is absent from the second-half Midpoint. Yet he's the protagonist of the story. It begins with him, and ends with him. All the turning points are driven by his decisions. He also has the longest internal journey to make. So how does it work dramatically for the second-half Midpoint to focus exclusively on another character's goal, conflict, and motivation?

While Rick is the protagonist of *Casablanca*, Ilsa is the stakes character. Whether he likes it or not, he's emotionally connected to her and what happens to her. In this way she serves as a type of surrogate for him in certain scenes, such as the second-half Midpoint. What happens to her and her goal of escaping Casablanca with Lazlo matters greatly to Rick, and that emotional connection is what pressures him to advance on his internal arc. Because if he doesn't change his attitudes and beliefs from cynicism to idealism, Ilsa will fail to achieve her goal and perish at the hands of Maj. Strasser. If he grows and changes, she will succeed. She personifies the consequences (or stakes) of Rick's internal journey.

The concept of a stakes character can also be used to telescope large-scale stakes into personalized consequences. This is particularly effective in "big" stories with large casts or several central characters who come and go in the story.

As in the Vietnam war bio-drama *We Were Soldiers*. Lt. Col. Hal Moore with 450 Americans are dropped in the middle of 2,000 battle-hardened Vietnamese Communists. The fight is extended and large-scale, involving swarms of mostly anonymous soldiers on both sides. If that was the only way the story played out, it would be easy to lose the audience's connection to what the men were feeling and experiencing. But early on in the battle a small platoon led by a promising young soldier is pinned down and Trapped. They're surrounded, outnumbered, outgunned. They're running out of water and ammunition. In every way they're facing the same external stakes Lt. Col. Moore is in the larger battle, only on a smaller, more personalized scale. And they're emotionally connected to Moore, because of his solemn vow before the battle began to never leave anyone behind, dead or alive. If they are Cut Off and lost, Moore will fail his internal journey of staying the course against all odds. At the 50% - 52.5% mark, Moore orders reinforcements to break through to the cut off men, but the Rescue (a variant of Escape) is blocked by an enemy ambush.

HIS OWN WORST ENEMY

If the protagonist sets a Trap at the first-half Midpoint, his incomplete knowledge likely causes him to overlook a hole in his plan or target the wrong person. Blinded by his own flaw, he unwittingly sets in motion the antagonist/villain's means to Escape.

As in Vera Caspary's romantic mystery *Laura*. While investigating the murder of a beautiful socialite, hardboiled police detective Mark McPherson falls in love with Laura posthumously. Then he discovers she's alive, the victim of mistaken identity. Determined to protect her from a second murder attempt, and jealous of her smarmy fiancé, Mark sets a Trap for the killer at the first-half Midpoint. He tests the shock value of Laura's resurrection from the dead first on an innocent servant, with emotionally shattering results. Convinced the plan will work, he then resets the Trap to snare his prime suspect: the fiancé. But at the 50% - 52.5% mark, Laura warns the fiancé in time for him to Escape incriminating himself, and Mark is forced to witness the couple's affectionate reunion. Mark's flawed behavior toward a loyal and innocent person at the first-half Midpoint motivates Laura's response in the second-half Midpoint, impressing upon Mark the necessity of changing his way of doing things if he's going to achieve his goal.

FURTHER READING

Suggestions to deepen your understanding of the Escape beat:

Kim Hudson's *The Virgin's Promise: Writing Stories of Feminine Creative, Spiritual and Sexual Awakening.* Chapter 4, "The Hero Archetypal Journey." Available in Kindle edition on Amazon and in print wherever books are sold.

Christopher Vogler's *The Writer's Journey: Mythic Structure for Writers.* Chapter, "Stage Eight: The Ordeal." Available in print on Amazon and wherever books are sold.

"Quick Look"

Attack

Hallmark: *An attack by the protagonist or antagonist exposes secret strengths, weaknesses, or alliances.*

Use an Attack in the second half of your Midpoint to...

- Increase tension when superior knowledge provided earlier to the reader is finally revealed to an invested character.
- Deliver valuable intelligence into the protagonist's hands concerning the antagonist's secret weapon or strength.
- Jeopardize an ally working undercover or expose a traitor in the ranks.
- Shine a public spotlight on the protagonist's motivations, forcing him to pick a side.
- Splinter the protagonist's team or alienate vital allies by exposing a moral weakness or failure.

(2nd Half) Attack

The protagonist dashes for the clearing's exit, but suddenly the ground erupts in front of him with a loud *bang!* He hits the dirt as searing flame and shrapnel from a grenade turns the air to a deadly haze. Ears ringing from the blast, limbs stinging from abrasions, he peers up through the roiling dust.

Across the glade stands a figure shimmering in outline. The villain! But not as the hero has ever seen him like before. The smoke from the attack has revealed his secret weapon—an invisibility cloak! Finally the protagonist knows exactly what he's up against.

The second-half Midpoint's Attack is often a big set piece, since attacks by definition are an aggressive act, usually involving weapons and violence, with the intent to kill or injure. But while it shares this surface feature with the first-half Midpoint Attack, its dramatic design and purpose differ significantly. This Attack forcibly exposes hidden agendas, identities, and alliances. In other words, Big Secrets. The person with the secret doesn't voluntarily share it here, either. It's torn out of their tight-fisted grip and dragged out into the open, catching them flatfooted and unprepared.

Stories of every kind benefit from characters with important secrets. Because it's human to have at least some secrets, it's an excellent tool to build three-dimensional characters and bring them to life. Anyone who's ever said, "But I've got nothing to hide," is deluding themselves. A secret doesn't necessarily have to be incriminating to be secret-worthy. It could simply involve self-preservation, protecting others, or living a normal life.

HIERARCHY OF SECRETS

Similar to Maslow's hierarchy of needs, there's a hierarchy of secrets. The ranking is not reflective of the secret's potential importance (that depends upon the character's motivation), but rather its distance or intimacy to the character's self-image and soul. Some secrets and their associated responsibilities can be transferred or passed on from one person to another, such as the combination to a top-secret vault. Other secrets remain one person's burden no matter how many people eventually discover the truth, such as a fear of being unworthy of love.

Physiological secrets concern food, shelter, sleep, etc. In *Panic in the Year Zero!* (1962), a middle-class American family on vacation flees nuclear holocaust and tries to survive in the mountains. The location of their food supply is an important secret. In David Robbins' dystopian *Endworld* series, the precise location of the protagonists' fortified retreat called the Home is carefully guarded to protect against an organized assault by their many enemies.

Secrets of safety concern the security of one's own physical person, employment, resources, family, health, and property. In Jennifer Crusie's romantic comedy *Welcome to Temptation*, the heroine arrives in town to secretly pen the script for a racy movie during the hero's mayoral reelection campaign. In Nora Roberts' romantic suspense *The Witness*, the heroine keeps her real identity as witness to a Russian mafia hit a secret even from the town sheriff she falls in love with. Like many superheroes, Oliver Queen in *Arrow* keeps the identity of his crime fighting alter ego secret from his friends, family, and ex-fiancee because he either can't trust them or to protect them from recrimination. In television series like *Burn Notice, Leverage,* and *Person of Interest*, the crime-fighting protagonists often guard their own secrets while simultaneously attempting to learn sensitive security information to expose the guilty and protect the innocent.

Secrets of love or belonging concern relationships with friends, family, and lovers. Of course, probably the most famous secret belonging to this category is Darth Vader's from *Star Wars V: The Empire Strikes Back* (1980): "I am your father." Followed a close second by *Chinatown*'s (1974) "She's my sister and my daughter!" But secrets concerning relationships aren't reserved for space operas or film noir. In the family drama series *McLeod's Daughters,* the heroine enlists the help of her hunky best friend to keep the true parentage of her unborn baby secret from her blackmailing ex-boyfriend.

Secrets of esteem concern achievement, respect of others, respect by others, recognition, and confidence. In *The Four Feathers* (1939), the protagonist, condemned and alienated by his lover and friends as a coward, adopts the guise of a beggar to win back their esteem. In the television series *Heartland*, horse-whisperer Amy Fleming practices perfecting a challenging equestrian routine in secret before revealing her mastery to family and professional associates.

Secrets of self-actualization concern morality, creativity, talents, and fulfillment. Fears of tangible things like snakes, spaces, or heights are great for short-term surprises but usually insufficient for story-length secrets. Fears of being controlled, of public failure, or of being inherently evil, are the juicy types of secrets closest and most intimate to the character. In *The Matrix* (1999) Neo believes he's keeping secret his extracurricular hacker talents. Television's favorite serial killer *Dexter* has a huge secret regarding his twisted morals.

UNWRAPPING THE LAYERS

Secrets seldom exist in isolation or solely on one plane. There are frequently layers of secrets wrapped around a core secret held closest to the character. For example, a woman on the run has the outer layer secret she's fleeing or hiding from someone. A deeper layer is her motive for running. Is it from guilt or self-preservation? Another layer is the identity of her pursuer. Is it cops or a bad boyfriend? Dig down to the heart of the matter, and her core secret may be shame for allowing herself to become involved in an abusive relationship.

Not all of this is exposed in one lump at the Midpoint. What makes secrets fun for readers is not only anticipating what the secret is, but the motivation behind it and the consequences (stakes) of its coming to light.

The key to revealing Big Secrets at the second-half Midpoint's Attack is how they are set up. Subordinate secrets wrapped around the Big Secret are peeled back bit by bit during the first half of the story. By the Midpoint, the reader has already learned what the basic Big Secret is, and therefore appreciates that exposing it will bring trouble to everyone concerned. The reader is probably not fully aware yet of the character's external motivation for it or internal core secret.

The point of the Attack is not revealing additional information to the *reader*, but rather to another character who will be significantly impacted by the secret. It's about repercussions and consequences. The other character (or characters) involved must respond to this new revelation or discovery, which comes as a world-changing shock to those who believed the secret-holder was on their side. Almost always the character's secret concerns an important alliance or loyalties at odds with other characters. A supposed ally is revealed as an enemy. An enemy turns out to be a friend.

The second-half Midpoint's Attack is one of the Big Reveals in a story, but certainly not the only or the last. The character who will be most impacted by the truth has yet to discover the secret-holder's deepest or darkest core secret. That comes later in the second half of the story. But for now at the Midpoint, there's enough trouble stirred up by unveiling the basic Big Secret to kick off the rest of the story with a vengeance.

VILLAN'S STRENGTH EXPOSED

The protagonist may launch an Attack against the villain, only to watch his best efforts go down in flames. However, in order to defeat the protagonist, the villain necessarily had to expose the existence of a secret weapon or capability. The protagonist may be worse off than he was before he lost the resources committed to his disastrous Attack, but he's learned something valuable about his enemy that can ultimately be used to turn the tables on him once and for all.

As in Robert A. Heinlein's science fiction classic *The Puppet Masters*. When earth is invaded by parasitic aliens known as the Masters, US government agent Sam goes undercover to assess the enemy. Based on his hard-won intelligence, the government gathers the military's best and strongest in a plan to wipe out the enemy hotspots. But at the first-half Midpoint, a Glimpse of a major city reveals to Sam the military is flying into a Trap. The aliens have taken over a much larger area of the nation than previously believed. At the 50% - 52.5% mark, Sam returns to Washington, D.C., but is too late to stop the military assault. He and the rest of the government leaders are forced to watch helplessly as

American forces are decimated or worse, disappear entirely into the alien ranks. The defeat reveals the aliens' secret ability to replicate at an astonishing rate, not only among human hosts, but also primate animals. Though much of America's military strength has been lost in the failed Attack, valuable insight into their enemy has been gained and they know better what they are up against.

The protagonist may urge someone else to Attack the villain in order to expose his opponent's secrets. He finds out at the Midpoint that responsibility for the success of his goal rests squarely on his own shoulders. No one else can and/or will do this job for him.

As in the Alfred Hitchcock classic, *Rear Window* (1954). At the 50% - 52.5% mark, Jeff (James Stewart) doubts witness statements that his neighbor put his missing wife, alive and well, on a train out of town. Frustrated, he urges his detective friend to go on the Attack and search the murderer's apartment. The detective, respecting the United States Constitution and his own professional future, refuses.

UNDERCOVER ALLY (OR TRAITOR)

The protagonist may successfully Attack the villain, only to unwittingly expose an unknown ally who was working undercover. It's not uncommon in espionage stories for interagency rivalry or lack of transparency to endanger undercover agents or assets unknowingly working on the same or similar cases. But this isn't limited to cloak and dagger spy stories.

In Suzanne Collins' dystopian fantasy *The Hunger Games,* Katniss and Peeta are selected to represent their district in a gladiatorial-style survival game. Despite the fact there can only be one winner, they bond as friends. He even declares his love for her, though she's unsure if it's genuine or pretend. When the Game begins, she feels betrayed to discover he's ganged up with rival tributes to hunt her down and eliminate her. At the first-half Midpoint, Peeta and the Career wolf pack Trap her up a tree, waiting to kill her at dawn. Then at the 50% - 52.5% mark, Katniss Attacks them with a deadly tracker-jacker nest, driving away her would-be killers and giving herself a short window to Escape. Except she's so badly stung she can't make a clean getaway before Peeta and another tribute return. "What are you still doing here? Are you mad? Run!" Peeta screams, and saves her life by throwing himself between her and the vicious tribute. The consequences of her successful Attack is that Peeta's true loyalty to her and betrayal of the Careers is exposed, resulting in their turning on him to kill him.

Katniss's first-person point-of-view in *The Hunger Games* limits the reader's awareness of Peeta's secret. The Big Reveal of his basic Big Secret—that he's really working *for* Katniss while pretending to work *against* her—occurs to the reader pretty much simultaneously when it occurs to the protagonist. However, Katniss's personality flaw of hardening herself against emotional vulnerability leaves the reader in the first half of the story with room for doubt concerning his apparent betrayal. There are hints the reader clings to in hope Peeta has a good reason for his behavior, a hope that's vindicated when Katniss's Attack triggers the Big Reveal.

It may be the villain's undercover- or double-agent who is exposed because of an Attack. He may have won the protagonist's trust in order to set him up for annihilation by the villain. He doesn't count on the protagonist's living to figure out the Judas's real identity and possibly return seeking revenge.

As in the classic romantic suspense *North By Northwest* (1959). When advertising executive Roger Thornhill (Cary Grant) is mistaken by foreign spies for a government agent, he's nearly killed and eventually framed for murder. On the run from spies and police, he finds unexpected refuge with a beautiful but mysterious woman on board a train. At the first-half Midpoint, Eve (Eva Marie Saint) pretends to helpfully arrange a meeting for him with the real government agent and bids him a hasty, emotional farewell. But when he arrives at the rendezvous, all he Glimpses is nothing but empty farmland in all directions. At the the 50% - 52.5% mark, a crop-dusting plane Attacks, strafing him with automatic weapons fire and driving him into a cornfield. The Attack reveals he's been set up by the woman he's fallen in love with.

Alfred Hitchcock is renowned as a master of suspense, and in *North By Northwest* he sets up the Big Reveal of Eve's basic Big Secret while Roger is still on the train. She sends a note to the villain a few compartments away, asking simply, "What do I do with him in the morning?" This lets the audience in on her basic Big Secret long before the second-half Midpoint's Attack clues in the unsuspecting protagonist. This allows the audience to wallow in suspense, wondering what kind of trouble is going to pounce on Roger out in the middle of nowhere. After he survives the Attack, he returns as a lover betrayed and determined to wrest answers from Eve, only to discover she's hiding more and bigger secrets, not only from him but also from the villain.

TRUTH WILL OUT

Sometimes the protagonist has been sitting on the fence regarding an issue, his loyalties divided between self and others. Perhaps he's in a situation because he cares about helping or protecting someone else, but at the same time a strong sense of self-preservation makes him want out. The second-half Midpoint's Attack can be the push that not only forces him to chose sides, but also makes his loyalties apparent to allies and enemies alike. Even if he's already committed to one side or the other, he may be pretending to be undecided or to sympathize with the other team in order to gain advantage.

As in the fourth season episode of the television spy series *Burn Notice*, "Breach of Faith." When Michael tries to help a desperate charity owner recover funds from a con man, he finds himself unwillingly involved in a hostage crisis. Surrounded by police, Michael's only hope of defusing the situation is to convince the hostages he's trying to help them, earn their trust, and get them to reveal where the stolen money's hidden. At the first-half Midpoint, he's temporarily Cut Off from backup, who are busy covering a separate mission across town. Then at the 50% - 52.5% mark, the villain grabs a gun from a desk drawer. Michael instinctively disarms him, foiling the Attack, and in so doing exposes his true loyalties. "You're not trying to help us! You're with him!" the villain exclaims, identifying Michael as his real opponent and "the one running the show."

SET UP FOR A FALL

An emotional Attack targeting the protagonist's morals or values at the first-half Midpoint may distract him from temporal danger, making him vulnerable for a physical Attack at the second-half Midpoint. Whether or not he succumbed to temptation, the second Attack may expose a perceived weakness or failing that alienates important allies.

As in David Thompson's Wilderness Series western, *Comanche Moon.* After legendary frontiersman Nate King rescues a greenhorn couple from a lustful mountain man and bloodthirsty Comanches, the trio are forced to set out on foot in a desperate attempt to reach civilization alive. At the first-half Midpoint, Cynthia makes a pass at Nate while he's alone one night on guard duty, and tries to convince him to betray his wife for her. Committed to his values and his marriage, he firmly rejects her every wile and argument. Distracted by a clever appeal to his flaw (a pride and passion for education), at the 50% - 52.5% mark, Nate lets down his guard for a moment. The mountain man Attacks and subdues Nate. Promising to make Nate suffer for perceived past wrongs, he first marches the mismatched couple over to awaken Cynthia's sleeping husband and expose their alleged secret infidelity. The reader knows the Big Secret that's revealed is actually a Big Lie, but there's just enough truth in it to have potentially disastrous consequences for Nate's and the couple's survival.

FURTHER READING

Suggestions to deepen your understanding of the Attack beat:

Ron Moskovitz's online article, "Dramatic Midpoints: Raising the Stakes." Currently available on The Script Lab: https://thescriptlab.com/features/screenwriting-101/1755-dramatic-midpoints-raising-the-stakes

Jeffrey Alan Schechter's online article, "Ask the Expert... Character Archetypes." Currently available on StoryLink at: http://www.storylink.com/article/319

Karen & The Babes' online article, "Kazza's List of Character 'Plots' and Secrets." Part One is currently available at: http://kgillsrpc.tumblr.com/post/36586432177/kazzas-list-of-character-plots-and-secrets . Part Two is currently available at: http://kgillsrpc.tumblr.com/post/37396011609/kazzas-list-of-character-plots-and-secrets-part-2

Mix and Match – Part 2

Suffocating humidity wraps around the snug little glade like a devouring python. Perspiration glistens on the protagonist's brow and rolls down his face. He thrashes helplessly against the ties that bind him to the central explosive tension, but you've done too good a job. The knots hold fast. He can't get away.

You twist the scarlet cord between your fingers, and move in to deliver the final touch to your Midpoint masterpiece.

The protagonist's eyes lock onto your hands, watching the loops take shape. "No, not another one. I can't take anymore."

A merciless smile curves your lips. "That's the whole point."

"Any more, and I'll be forced to... *change!*"

"You'll thank me later."

Just like the first-half Midpoint, each of the four beats that may appear at the second-half Midpoint—Questions & Answers, Love vs. Goal, Escape, and Attack—can stand alone or double up. Long stories supporting important subplots may have the page count to provide pairs of beats their own separate scenes. Average-length stories more commonly pair beats within a single event.

At the second-half Midpoint, the most popular mix-and-match concerns one beat triggering or leading into the next beat for the same character. Most often, although not always, that character is the protagonist. He's the one on the journey to accomplish the story goal, and he's the one who must change internally in order to achieve his desire. So after the event(s) of the first-half Midpoint slap him awake to this awareness that change is not only inevitable, it's upon him right now!—the second-half Midpoint focuses on his response. Will he embrace a higher moral value and change the way he's doing things, setting the story on course for a hard-won but happy ending? Or will he reject higher values and determinedly dig himself even deeper into a hole of his own making, setting the story on course for a satisfying but unhappy resolution?

The latter decision belongs to some modern literary fiction and cautionary tales like Mario Puzo's *The Godfather* or J.R.R. Tolkien's *The Children of Hurin*. Although those types of stories resonate powerfully with a certain devoted audience, in cultures shaped by Judeo-Christian influences the larger marketshare is enjoyed by stories celebrating hope and redemption.

EXTERNAL GOAL

The Midpoint tug of war on the protagonist's heart can spin his external goal around in a completely different though related direction. Deciding between Love versus Goal can lead him to change his objective from pursuing a specific outcome to trying to Escape the same outcome. Unravelling his earlier successes are guaranteed to prove a major headache. Pitting the protagonist against an outdated version of his own external goal is a great way to contrast the protagonist's pre-Midpoint values against his post-Midpoint values.

As in the romantic comedy blockbuster *While You Were Sleeping* (1995). Lucy's happily-ever-after fantasies about a certain handsome stranger come weirdly to life when she saves his life during a mugging and his boisterous family mistakenly adopt her as his "fiancee." At the first-half Midpoint, a sweetly innocent walk home with his brother reveals a Glimpse of what real love looks like. Her old dreams of Peter pale in comparison to the reality of her feelings for Jack. Then at the 50% - 52.5% mark, Lucy's challenged to choose between her newly recognized real Love for Jack versus her old Goal of clinging to the fantasy of marrying Peter. She happily chooses Love, but Midpoints are never about making life easier for the protagonist, even if it's an upbeat moment. Since Jack will never betray his family's happiness by poaching on his comatose brother's girlfriend, the only hope she has of winning his love requires Escaping the deception she successfully crafted in the first half of the story.

Even when one beat leads into the next *without* altering the protagonist's goal, the one-two punch can significantly change the way the protagonist goes about pursuing his goal. Primal story goals like survival are unlikely to change very much, even at major turning points. Perhaps during the first part of the story his goal was to keep his head down and stay out of the line of fire, merely trying to survive until everything blows over. However, the Midpoint snaps him out of his defensive posture and ignites an offensive Attack plan. He realizes he isn't going to achieve his goal of survival without taking the war to the enemy.

As in Suzanne Collins' dystopian fantasy *The Hunger Games*. Katniss knows when she volunteers to take her kid sister's place in the government-mandated gladiatorial Hunger Games that her chances of survival are nil, but that doesn't prevent her giving it her best shot. Once the games begin, she's on the run, trying to stay one step ahead of a "wolf pack" hunting her down to kill her. At the first-half Midpoint, they Trap her up a tree, waiting to finish her off at dawn. One way or another, her days of playing the Game on the defense are over. Then at the 50% - 52.5% mark, she launches a successful surprise Attack against them and Escapes. From this point on, she goes on the offensive and takes the fight to the enemy, which ultimately includes the aloof entities cold-bloodedly orchestrating the Game. She realizes winning her life is going to require taking risks and laying it on the line.

INTERNAL CONFLICT

Instead of cascading in a cause-and-effect scenario, beats may clash and get in one another's way, emphasizing and heightening the protagonist's internal conflict. Perhaps the protagonist tries to employ a beat in furtherance of his external goal, but another beat won't let him make progress unless he examines his own soul first.

As in James Oliver Curwood's *The Flaming Forest.* RMCP David Carrigan won't give up until he gets his man, even when it means suffering gunshot and kidnapping by a beautiful woman. Marie-Anne claims to be the wife of his prime suspect, a renowned river man known as St. Pierre. At the first-half Midpoint, David recounts the official version of his prey's crimes, but this false Glimpse does nothing to sway her loyalty. However, a later Glimpse of true love with Marie-Anne in his arms leaves him shaken to the core. At the 50% - 52.5% mark, her husband's return is greeted with celebration by his people. David spies on the couple's public reunion, trying to observe Answers to his Questions both about the man and the couple's relationship. But his newly realized love for Marie-Anne gets in the way of his professional assessment of St. Pierre, obscuring truths about his rival's strength and character. It's not until he guiltily acknowledges and deals with this internal conflict of Love vs. Goal that he can take an accurate measure of the real man.

A LIFELINE OF HOPE

Sometimes a beat delivers failure to the protagonist's doorstep, triggering his resorting to another beat in order to regroup or make sense out of defeat. When something so devastating happens at the Midpoint that it seems this could be a harbinger of how the story ends, both the protagonist and reader need a lifeline thrown to them promising a way out. It doesn't matter how thin the lifeline is. The reader will attach their anticipation to a single thread of hope.

As in Robert A. Heinlein's science fiction classic *The Puppet Masters.* Government agent Sam spearheads the United States' intelligence response to an alien invasion by the Masters. While military forces gather for a massive strike against alien hotspots, he scouts Kansas City at the first-half Midpoint. To his horror, he Glimpses a major metropolis presumed "clean" completely overrun by the enemy. At the 50% - 52.5% mark, he flies back to Washington, D.C., but is too late to prevent the doomed Attack and resulting loss of America's best and strongest military forces. Reeling from the disaster, Sam visits a government laboratory for Answers to how the enemy outnumbered them so quickly and by such a huge margin.

Of course, these beats can be shuffled into any logical order desired. Perhaps the protagonist's Q & A is interrupted by the villain's Attack. In which case, the dynamic of hope is reversed. The Midpoint event starts out in the protagonist's favor, but his hopes for a quick and positive resolution wind up dashed.

As in the James Bond spy thriller *Dr. No* (1962). Investigating the disappearance of a scientist and disrupted Cape Canaveral space launches, at the first-half Midpoint 007 slips out of a Trap set for him by a femme fatale. Then at the 50% - 52.5% mark, he gets the drop on his would-be assassin and interrogates him for Answers about the scientist's fate. The assassin dives for a gun and Attacks. Bond is forced to kill the man in self-defense before ascertaining the identity of the villainous mastermind pulling the strings.

ANTAGONIST IN CHARGE

Sometimes the antagonist wields a beat like a cattle prod on the protagonist, provoking him to respond with another beat. The protagonist may have considered throwing in the towel and giving up on his external goal because the price of internal change was too high or seemed out of reach. But the antagonist's move compels him to reengage the story.

As in Debbie Macomber's contemporary romance *The Way to a Man's Heart.* Literature professor Grey is comfortable in his dull, predictable life until he meets and falls for effervescent waitress Meghan. At the first-half Midpoint, he sees her chatting innocently with a younger man and jumps to the conclusion he's Glimpsing an inevitable future where she grows tired of him and dumps him. Despairing he can ever change his stodgy ways, he preemptively Cuts Off their relationship to avoid further pain. But at the 50% - 52.5% mark, Meghan bursts into his office wanting Answers. Why did he suddenly quit liking her when she thought they'd found something special? Faced with Grey's stony response, her Questions wither on her lips, and she slinks away, rejected. But her visit generates Questions of his own, and the need for Answers compels Grey to track her down later at the diner. Why did she search him out at his office when she could have moved on with her pick of any young man?

Occasionally the second-half Midpoint turns everything on its head by handing both reins to the antagonist or villain. Because the Midpoint as a whole is all about cause-and-effect, braiding together the external goal with internal change, in cases like this the first-half Midpoint must be driven by the protagonist. The antagonist cannot be the only driver of *both* halves of the Midpoint, otherwise he will take over the story and the protagonist will suffer an unbelievably huge hole in his character arc. So after the protagonist gives it his best shot at the first-half Midpoint, the villain may swoop in at the second-half Midpoint to flex his muscles and try to intimidate the protagonist into giving up.

As in the romantic wartime classic *Casablanca* (1942). Rick's (Humphrey Bogart) cynical facade cracks right down the middle the moment old flame Ilsa (Ingrid Bergman) walks into his nightclub on the arm of renowned resistance leader Lazlo (Paul Henreid). Desperate to escape the Nazis, at the first-half Midpoint Ilsa appeals to Rick for help, going so far as trying to give him a Glimpse of the real reason she jilted him. But in his pain, he cruelly Cuts Off her explanation, and she leaves in tears. At the 50% - 52.5% mark, Lazlo and Ilsa (in the role of stakes character and dramatic surrogate for the protagonist) appear before Maj. Strasser, the evil Nazi villain of the story. He grills the couple with Questions, alternately bribing or threatening them to give up the names of other resistance workers, but in vain. Their chances of successfully Escaping the country are openly discussed—and rejected—by Maj. Strasser, who smugly reveals the corrupt local authorities are firmly in his pocket.

Tools for Crafting Midpoint Beats

A great blue heron croaks harshly as it takes flight, and the shadow of wide wings sweeps gracefully across the humid clearing in the Great Swampy Middle. You push the Indiana Jones-style fedora back on your forehead, scrutinizing the explosive central tension one final time before setting it off.

A niggling worry trickles down your spine. There are so many options and possible combinations, how can you be sure you made the best choice for the story?

Remembering the satchel slung across your chest, you dig out your demolition tools. "Many threads of the hero's history lead in, and many threads of possibility and change lead out the other side." (Vogler 160) You test each of the loops of fuse tied in a big red bow to the bomb. It only takes a few moments, and when you're finished you nod to yourself in confident satisfaction.

Letting your imagination run wild and experimenting with various beats at the Midpoint is a great way to find the special twist that can elevate a story from good to great. But there are times when a multitude of options pushes creativity over the edge into confusion.

Once the writer has explored all the beat options, it's time to narrow down those choices to only the ones that best serve the story.

Three simple tools exist to whittle any beat down to its essential components, so the writer can instantly recognize whether or not it's the best fit for his story.

Tool #1

Which characters are involved?

If the protagonist has any kind of a character arc, then it's a given he belongs in the primary beat at the first and/or second half of the Midpoint. Usually he appears in both. Even if he's physically absent from one of them, he's still the central focus.

In *The Adventures of Robin Hood* (1938), the first-half Midpoint beat involves Prince John and his evil henchmen plotting to Trap the roguish outlaw. Robin Hood isn't anywhere around, but the whole beat points the audience's attention toward him. The other characters are directing all their conversation, their thoughts, their intentions toward the protagonist.

It builds tension by investing superior knowledge in the audience concerning a feared outcome for their beloved archer. When Robin Hood shows up in the second-half Midpoint beat confident he can Escape anything his enemies throw at him, the audience hopes his swagger is justified and fears it's not.

In *Casablanca* (1942), Rick (the protagonist) defeats Ilsa (the antagonist) in the first-half Midpoint by cruelly Cutting Off the backstory Glimpse she tries to reveal. The second-half Midpoint confrontation with Maj. Strasser (the villain) about her and Victor's intended Escape is left to her. Rick is elsewhere, probably sleeping off the effects of an alcoholic binge.

The other character whose presence is required at the first and/or second half Midpoint beats is the antagonist. Why? He's the character who intentionally applies pressure on the protagonist to change. He knows how to make it personal, too.

Even if he doesn't physically step on stage in one of the beats, he's going to be the center of attention. He's a danger to the protagonist's equilibrium, and threats must be dealt with.

In Debbie Macomber's *Rainy Day Kisses*, the hero (the antagonist) takes the heroine (the protagonist) on a date in the park to fly kites at the first-half Midpoint. It's a Glimpse for her of what love and life could be like. At the second-half Midpoint, although the hero is physically absent, he's the focal point of the heroine's Q & A with her married sister about love and romance.

Some stories have both an antagonist and a villain. While the antagonist's role is to apply pressure to the protagonist to change, the villain's role is to pressure him to fail. Both roles are concerned with intentional and personal *opposition* to the protagonist's specific external and/or internal goals.

Unlike antagonists, villains are morally evil or at least estranged in their hearts from the Judeo-Christian moral code of right and wrong. Whether they embrace religion, agnosticism, or atheism, their mastery of rationalization enables them to legitimize anything they want to do, regardless of the harm to others. They are essentially their own higher moral authority. The villain, more than any other character in the story, personifies the dark potential of the protagonist if he fails to grow and change.

If a story has a villain, he needs to make an appearance at the Midpoint, too. In *Casablanca* (1942), the antagonist is Ilsa. She shows up in the first-half of the Midpoint, opposing the protagonist's cynical perception of the past. Maj. Strasser is the villain, and he shows up in the second-half of the Midpoint. He blocks the antagonist from leaving the story, and compels her to reengage with the protagonist.

In mysteries, the villain's appearance at the Midpoint is almost never perceived as villainous by the protagonist or supporting characters. Their attention is usually centered so hard and fast on another suspect that they fail to recognize the significance of the villain's appearance. Later, when the protagonist is further along on his character arc, he will look back at the Midpoint and—*click!*—the pieces will fit together.

In Vera Caspary's *Laura*, the cop protagonist suspects Laura's fiance of the murder, partly out of jealousy and partly because the fiance acts like he's hiding something. At the first-half Midpoint, the protagonist uses the antagonist (the romantic interest, Laura herself) to set a Trap. At the second-half Midpoint, he prepares to spring it on the fiance, but who should unexpectedly step into it instead? The villain! However, the protagonist is focused so hard on not letting the fiance Escape, he's blind to the significance of the villain's tell-tale reaction.

Caspary's novel has a strong romantic subplot, but is above all a mystery. The movie version shifted the story structure to emphasize the romantic element. The Midpoint becomes less about catching the murderer and more about bringing the central romantic couple closer together. The villain still makes an unexpected appearance, although the circumstances are entirely different from those in the book. Once again, the protagonist's attention is focused elsewhere so he misses the walking, talking clue barging into the scene. (For detailed analysis of the movie version's Midpoint, please see the chapter, "Additional Examples from Novels, TV, & Movies.")

Tool #2

What activity does the character perform?

While more than merely a "plot point," the Midpoint's impact upon the plot is every bit as great as upon the character's internal development. In fact, leveraging the forces of plot is precisely *how* the Midpoint accomplishes such a big step in the protagonist's internal change.

So what is plot? It's the protagonist's motivated pursuit of a goal despite opposition. The goal changes and grows as he deals with obstacles and complications along the way, but the goal keeps him active and moving forward in the story.

If there is no forward movement at the Midpoint in the external plot, then there's no reason for the character to advance on his internal arc. Thus, something big and tangible to the character's physical senses needs to happen here. This is not the time for navel-gazing. It's the time for action!

Be careful the "something big" doesn't only happen *to* the protagonist. Certainly the antagonist or villain initiates certain beats at the Midpoint, but the protagonist must be active in the plot, too. If the antagonist cuts him off at the pass, it's because the protagonist is pursuing a certain course of action the antagonist wants stopped. If the antagonist traps or attacks him, it's because he needs to stop the protagonist from doing what he's doing.

The antagonist has no motive to stop the protagonist if the protagonist is doing nothing. So make sure he's doing something related to his goal, the same goal the antagonist opposes at all costs.

It's essential to keep in mind that the antagonist has a goal which he actively pursues, too. It's just as important to him and he's just as committed to it as the protagonist is to his own. Maybe even more so. The Midpoint is often just as much of a test of his commitment and how far he will go to attain what he wants as it is for the protagonist.

Activity, although external, means different things in different genres and stories. In the romantic comedy *While You Were Sleeping* (1995), at the Midpoint the characters take a romantic nighttime walk in the snow. They don't even kiss! But in the plot it's a pivotal love scene, and it's an external action that advances and swivels the story in a new direction.

In J.R.R. Tolkien's epic fantasy *The Hobbit*, Bilbo fights wicked spiders in Mirkwood forest and rescues his friends from being eaten alive. Pretty exciting, but it's also an external action that keeps the story moving forward and swivels the relationship dynamics in a new direction.

Even when the protagonist at the Midpoint gives up and quits the story, the act of packing up his marbles and heading home is activity. He doesn't merely think about doing it. He does it.

In Debbie Macomber's contemporary romance *The Way to a Man's Heart*, when the hero sees the heroine with another man, he doesn't just consider breaking up with her. He breaks up with her! Of course he doesn't actually make it back to his old, ivy-covered hobbit hole before the antagonist comes after him to drag him back into the story.

Protagonists aren't the only characters subject to fits of despair. Antagonists may temporarily decide their goal's not worth the heartache and try to cut their losses by quitting the story at the Midpoint, too.

In the TV series *Once Upon a Time*, Belle walks out on Rumplestiltskin (aka The Beast), even though she's in love with him, because she senses something evil inside him. The Evil Queen waylays her and convinces her to give the relationship another shot. (For detailed analysis of this popular episode's Midpoint, please see the chapter, "Additional Examples from Novels, TV, & Movies.")

If either the protagonist or antagonist attempts to quit the story, they usually do so at the first-half Midpoint. This sets up the activity at the second-half Midpoint to concentrate on them changing their minds, recommitting to their goal, and reengaging with the story.

Tool #3

What discovery or decision does the character make?

If you've seen one explosion, you've seen them all. And a kiss is, after all, just a kiss. The way to make familiar scenes fresh and original, engaging both the characters' and reader's emotions, is by detailing the discovery or decision that causes it to happen.

This tool connects the character's arc with the action in the plot, infusing activity with thematic relevance and meaning. Action by itself can devolve into mindless repetition, with no real alteration to the character's situation. However, specific action triggered by a discovery or decision necessarily produces a meaningful change in the story and a genuine turning point.

A kiss becomes more than just another kiss in TV's *Once Upon a Time* when it's triggered by the Prince's discovery that true love's kiss can break any curse. The new knowledge triggers a breathless gallop to resurrect his true love, Snow White, from her deathless eternal sleep. The highest stakes of all—life and death—hang suspended on that kiss. It reveals the true depths of their feelings and commitment to each other.

Discoveries are essential to creating the kinds of upside-down reversals and surprising twists that compel readers to turn pages faster and faster. Karl Iglesias in *Writing for Emotional Impact* says, "Obviously, for something to be discovered, first it must be hidden." (103) Controlling information flow to the reader is essential to setting up the discovery or revelation. Unlike suspense, which relies upon the reader's awareness of a specific threat, surprises are effectively set up by concealing pertinent information. "The best way to do so is to leave events off-screen, which makes their discovery emotionally satisfying." (104)

It's also important to play fair with the reader, especially if the knowledge that's discovered was withheld by a point-of-view character. Whatever the character would logically think about at any given time while the story's in his POV, the reader must be privy to also.

However, there are tricks a writer can employ. If the character's thoughts veer toward the secret, he may shut them down because emotionally he "doesn't want to go there." Or he can be distracted by an external stimulus, such as an interruption by another character or even a phone ringing.

Take care not to overuse the same device or resort to cliches. Interruptions turn into cliches if they happen by coincidence, so instead imbue them with purpose and intent. If a ringing phone interrupts the POV character's thought processes from spilling the beans to the reader, that phone call better get the character into more trouble, not out of trouble. That way, the reader has more to worry about than what the character's hiding.

An explosion becomes more than another ball of fire in TV's *Breaking Bad* when it's triggered by a science teacher's decision to gain restitution from the local drug distributor for his partner's brutal beating and the theft of their meth. The decision, committed to and translated into corresponding action, not only raises the stakes in the external plot but reveals new depths of character. How far will the protagonist go? What values will he reject or embrace? Now the audience knows, all because of a decision that yields action.

Sometimes the order is switched around, and action triggers the character's decision. David Howard in *How to Build a Great Screenplay* says, "An outside impediment prompts an internal decision, or a decision brings the character up against an outside force." (20) What matters is that the action or decision turns the character's path in a new, unexpected direction.

Even the simplest decisions are based on value judgments, which are informed by attitudes and experiences accumulated throughout life. Dwight V. Swain in *Techniques of the Selling Writer* says decisions depend on the character's personality and background, their emotional and intellectual patterns. (183) Put simply, decisions drive the plot, but characterization drives the decisions.

Howard says, "Each time we are with a character who faces a new obstacle [and] makes a decision… it strengthens our bond with the character. It makes us care more." (21) He explains that decisions provide the reader with a window into the character's soul and its true inner workings. When life tosses a monkey wrench at the protagonist, he's caught off guard. The old pretenses and defense mechanisms that worked to support the status quo are unsuited for handling increased stakes. The character has to quickly change how he responds. In that moment when he's scrambling to make a decision, his true nature and what he really values is exposed to the reader.

The truest test of a character's arc is to ask, "What did he do at the end that he never would or could have done at the beginning?" The decision the character makes at the Midpoint is an essential stepping stone in that internal progression from "Never in a million years!" to "I'm ready, willing, and able."

The Midpoint decision signals to the reader a tipping point in the protagonist's values, attitudes, and life experiences. In the first half of the story, the scales are heavily weighted in favor of defending the status quo endangered by the antagonist and events in the plot. At the Midpoint the character is finally convinced there's enough weight on the other side of the scales to risk changing either his goal or his method of pursuing it. Though his journey will not be complete until the final climax of the story, the decision at the Midpoint is what makes the ending possible.

PUTTING THE TOOLS TO WORK

When auditioning beats for your story's Midpoint, first consider which of the main characters are going to be present in the scenes. Ideally, at least one of the beats needs to pit the protagonist and antagonist against each other in a direct and personal confrontation.

Remember "confrontation" doesn't necessarily mean angry scenes brimming with negative emotions. It could mean a carefree walk in the park. How it's expressed on the page is a matter of interpretation and the unique requirements of the story. What matters is there's a beat somewhere at the Midpoint where the antagonist's opposition to the protagonist's flaw finally compels the protagonist to change either his goal or his way of pursuing it.

If the protagonist and antagonist absolutely cannot logically appear in the same scene together, then their respective beats need to concentrate on each other. The protagonist's beat should focus on the absent antagonist. The antagonist's beat should focus on the absent protagonist.

If there's a villain, he most certainly makes an appearance. If the protagonist is AWOL or otherwise occupied when the villain shows up, a surrogate or stakes character can come in handy. The stakes character acts as an emotional extension of the protagonist's interests. The villain can put the stakes character in intense jeopardy at the Midpoint, even kill him without ending the story, while the reader anticipates the reflected hurt suffered by the protagonist.

Focus the Midpoint beats on these characters: the protagonist and antagonist. A villain (if the story has one). And possibly a stakes character (if appropriate). Sometimes a character inhabits more than one role. In *Casablanca* (1942), Ilsa is the antagonist to Rick in one scene. In the next scene, she dons the role of stakes character against the villain.

Keeping the function of their dramatic roles in mind, take a moment to jot down the names of the primary characters involved in each beat of your story's Midpoint.

Keep the characters active. Give them something physical to do that advances the plot. It will inject energy into the scenes, and externalize the motivating forces behind the protagonist's resulting character development.

Depending on the story and characters, the beats' main action could be anything—a big, splashy "set piece" or a quiet conversation. Dialogue, when well-done, is action, too. Interesting characters don't merely talk to each other. They use their words to brag, praise, threaten, comfort, etc., in pursuit of a personally-meaningful agenda. That agenda is no less intentional if it's selfish or unselfish. In *Casablanca* (1942), both halves of the Midpoint contain beats wherein the characters do no more than sit down and have a conversation. But those conversations advance the plot (and the characters!) because the dialogue is doing something—it's actively pleading, insulting, bribing, defying, threatening, etc.

Of course, some stories may require a big, intense, even violent Midpoint beat. When that's so, make it the biggest, the most intense, and the bloodiest yet. In *Star Wars IV: A New Hope* (1977), the villain doesn't blast some paltry space rocks. He blows up an entire planet and everyone on it! In *The Hunt for Red October* (1990), the Soviet attack plane doesn't fire warning shots at the protagonist's submarine. It launches torpedoes to sink that high-tech tin can to the bottom of the ocean! In Robert A. Heinlein's *The Puppet Masters*, the United States doesn't issue sanctions against the occupied territories. It throws its best and heaviest military resources, everything it's got, at the alien invaders!

What does the character put on the line that he's never risked before? His career? His heart? His life? Keeping those stakes in mind, jot down the activity the characters perform in each beat of your story's Midpoint.

To be genuinely meaningful, whatever activity the character is involved in needs to be connected to a discovery or decision. Either the discovery/decision triggers the action, or the action triggers the discovery/decision. What matters is that the discovery or decision elevates the Midpoint action above every other preceding action, making it different in some significant way.

Maybe the action compels the character to alter his decision-making process, even reassess what he values most or is willing to give up. Or maybe a discovery forces the character to take an action previously beyond his limits of consideration.

At the Midpoint something changes within the core of the character, and that change is externalized for the reader in the symbiotic unity of action and discovery/decision. While a discovery or decision imbues action with depth and meaning, action provides the discovery or decision with urgency and proof of intent.

In real life, people may discover new information or make a decision and then drag their feet about responding. Characters are seldom if ever allowed that luxury, and never at the Midpoint. The action at the Midpoint either supplies the urgency to respond *now*, or (if the discovery/decision triggers the action) convinces the reader of the character's sincerity of purpose.

Jot down what the character discovers or decides to do that makes an *immediate* difference to the story's trajectory in each Midpoint beat.

The following is an example of applying these three tools to the Midpoint beats in the Old Testament story of Queen Esther. The Biblical book of Esther records the historical origin of the Jewish feast of Purim, but it's also a classic Cinderella tale spiced with a genocidal villain. There are two beats in the first half of the Midpoint, occurring at Esther 5:1-6, and two beats in the second half of the Midpoint, occurring at Esther 5:6-11.

First Half

BEAT: Glimpse

CHARACTERS: Queen Esther and the king.

ACTIVITY: Queen Esther risks execution to enter the palace's forbidden inner court, seeking an audience with the king.

DISCOVERY/DECISION: The king decides to not only spare Esther's life, but offers to grant her any request, even half of his kingdom.

BEAT: Trap

CHARACTERS: Queen Esther and the king.

ACTIVITY: Queen Esther sets a trap for her secret enemy by offering a personal dinner invitation to the king and his royal advisor, Haman.

DISCOVERY/DECISION: Charmed, the king and Haman decide to hurry to Esther's banquet.

Second Half

BEAT: Q & A

CHARACTERS: Queen Esther and the king.

ACTIVITY: At the banquet, the king questions Esther to find out what she really wants.

DISCOVERY/DECISION: Esther decides to explain everything at a second banquet the following night.

BEAT: Escape

CHARACTERS: Haman and Mordecai.

ACTIVITY: On his way home from the banquet, Haman can't avoid his ancestral enemy, Mordecai, and becomes furious when the dignified Jew refuses to tremble subserviently.

DISCOVERY/DECISION: Haman discovers his great wealth and high position is worth nothing to him so long as Mordecai lives.

FURTHER READING

Suggestions to deepen your understanding of these tools:

David Howard's *How to Build a Great Screenplay: A Master Class in Storytelling for Film.* Chapter One, "The Story." A great examination of discovery and decision. Available in ebook and print on Amazon and wherever books are sold.

Robert McKee's *Story: Substance, Structure, Style, and the Principles of Screenwriting.* Chapter 11, "Scene Analysis." Using a smaller definition of "beats" that means action/reaction behavior units within a scene, McKee offers superb instruction on activating dialogue. Available in ebook and print on Amazon and wherever books are sold.

For a helpful visualization aid of the Midpoint beats, please turn to the next page...

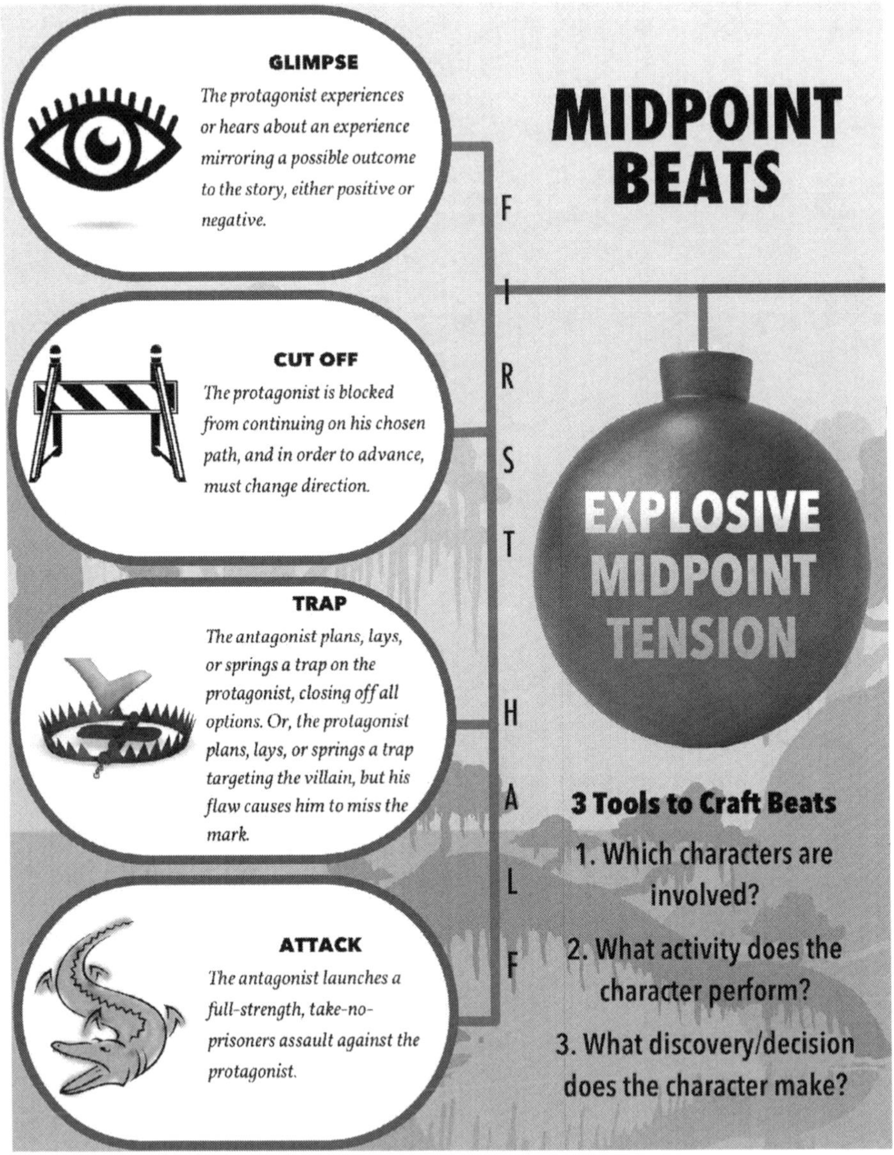
MIDPOINT BEATS
GLIMPSE
The protagonist experiences or hears about an experience mirroring a possible outcome to the story, either positive or negative.
CUT OFF
The protagonist is blocked from continuing on his chosen path, and in order to advance, must change direction.
TRAP
The antagonist plans, lays, or springs a trap on the protagonist, closing off all options. Or, the protagonist plans, lays, or springs a trap targeting the villain, but his flaw causes him to miss the mark.
ATTACK
The antagonist launches a full-strength, take-no-prisoners assault against the protagonist.
FIRST HALF
EXPLOSIVE MIDPOINT TENSION
3 Tools to Craft Beats
1. Which characters are involved?
2. What activity does the character perform?
3. What discovery/decision does the character make?

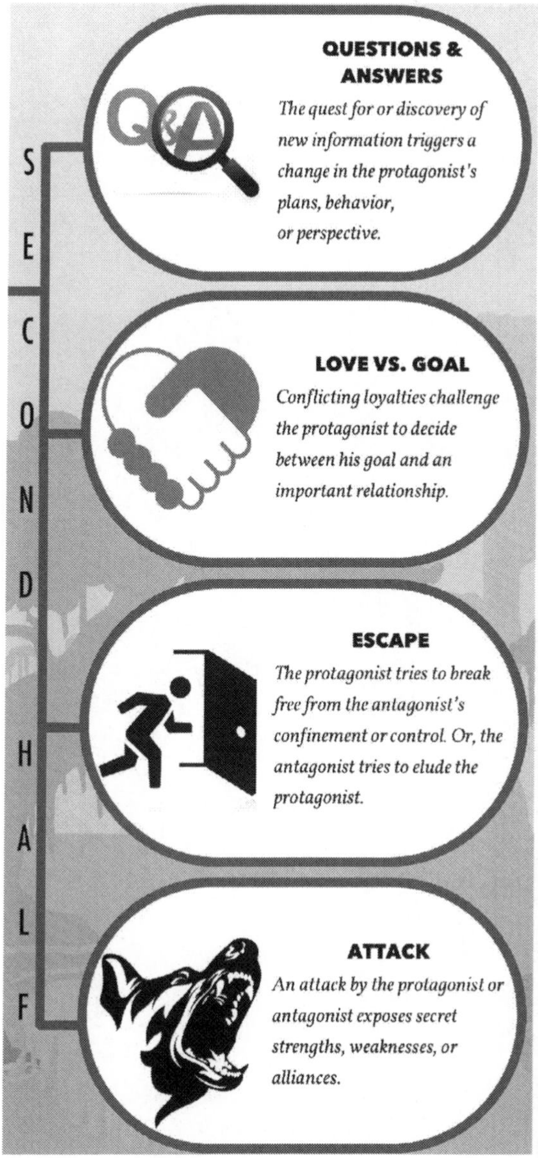
SECOND HALF
QUESTIONS & ANSWERS
Q&A
The quest for or discovery of new information triggers a change in the protagonist's plans, behavior, or perspective.
LOVE VS. GOAL
Conflicting loyalties challenge the protagonist to decide between his goal and an important relationship.
ESCAPE
The protagonist tries to break free from the antagonist's confinement or control. Or, the antagonist tries to elude the protagonist.
ATTACK
An attack by the protagonist or antagonist exposes secret strengths, weaknesses, or alliances.

EXAMPLE

TESS OF THE STORM COUNTRY

by Grace Miller White

First Half

BEAT: Attack
CHARACTERS: Tess, Frederick, & Ben
ACTIVITY: Ben breaks into Tess' shanty at night to abduct her, but Frederick saves her.
DISCOVERY/DECISION: Tess decides Frederick is a worthy protector.

BEAT: Glimpse
CHARACTERS: Tess & Frederick
ACTIVITY: A passionate kiss turns Tess and Frederick into lovers.
DISCOVERY/DECISION: Tess discovers love is the great equalizer between classes.

Second Half

BEAT: Q & A
CHARACTERS: Tess & Frederick
ACTIVITY: Frederick confides he's hiding from prankster college sophomores.
DISCOVERY/DECISION: Tess discovers he's not running from the law.

BEAT: Escape
CHARACTERS: Tess & Dan Jordan
ACTIVITY: Tess arranges a covert meeting with Frederick's college buddy, Dan Jordan.
DISCOVERY/DECISION: Tess decides on a plan to help Frederick evade the college sophomores.

Additional Examples from Novels, TV, & Movies

Alias. Season two, episode thirteen, "Phase One."

Airing after Super Bowl XXXVII, this J.J. Abrams-penned episode scored big for the spy thriller series in every way. The Midpoint is a perfectly executed balance of action-driven main plot and character-driven subplot, setting up the personal stakes for a tragic twist at the end. It's a great example of interpreting the same beat in entirely different ways and mirroring them within the same Midpoint event.

First half of the Midpoint — At the 47.5% - 50% mark, the protagonist Sydney GLIMPSES her two best friends, Will and Francie, acting strangely during dinner. They confess their friendship has unexpectedly leaped to the next level, and they're romantically involved. Meanwhile, back at the office, the villain Geiger tries to get a GLIMPSE at a coworker's keylog record to ferret out the identity of a suspected double-agent.

Second half of the Midpoint — At the 50% - 52.5% mark, after dinner a delighted Sydney subjects Will to a friendly Q & A about his relationship with Francie. He doesn't know where it's heading, but it doesn't feel weird. It feels rather wonderful. Meanwhile, Geiger gets the answers he's seeking when he recovers erased text from an email revealing Sydney and her father are double agents. (Q & A)

Arrow. Season one, episode twenty-three, "Sacrifice."

Here's a rare example of a Midpoint devoid of the protagonist or even a surrogate stakes character. The key to why it works is understanding its position in the larger story arc of the season. It occurs at the very end of the final "sequence" of episodes. The protagonist has already confronted the villain and was soundly defeated in the previous episode. Now he digs deep down to make the ultimate sacrifice for what he believes. The strength of his conviction inspires other characters to embrace key turning points of their own, setting various story lines on a collision course with Oliver Queen's effort to save thousands of innocent lives from destruction.

First half of the Midpoint — At the 47.5% - 50% mark, Moira Queen holds a press conference exposing a conspiracy to ATTACK a section of the city known as the Glades. She identifies fellow mogul Malcolm Merlyn as the master schemer who extorted her complicity in the plot. Claiming to possess proof of his crimes, she implicates him in several murders. (GLIMPSE unmasking her personal vulnerability and the villain's strengths.)

Second half of the Midpoint — At the 50% - 52.5% mark, Moira warns everyone in the Glades to ESCAPE and surrenders to police arrest, but her daughter rushes into the heart of danger to rescue her boyfriend. Hearing Moira's confession on television, an incredulous Tommy demands his father tell him the truth about the murders. (Q&A) Malcolm is unrepentant in the face of his son's outrage: "I did what I had to do."

The Avengers (2012)

Even in ensemble pieces, one character's arc will stand out from the rest at pivotal moments. In this case, it's Romanoff (Scarlett Johannson). At the Midpoint she alone confronts the villain, gets the job done, and keeps the story moving. This example also presents an interesting spin on revealing backstory. The protagonist usually uses a Glimpse of backstory and personal vulnerability to build trust and connection. Here Romanoff uses the backstory Glimpse to Trap the villain into revealing the truth, correctly assessing his megalomaniacal and predatory nature will seek to exploit any perceived weakness.

First half of the Midpoint — At the 47.5% - 50% mark, Romanoff confronts Loki in his holding cell to inquire about Agent Barton. He wonders why she's more concerned about one man than the whole world. She confesses to owing Agent Barton a debt for sparing her life and recruiting her to work for S.H.I.E.L.D. Loki knows the GLIMPSE of her backstory is incomplete, and cruelly fills in the bloody blanks until she appears emotionally destroyed. He brags about how he'll hurt her and those she cares about—a GLIMPSE of his plans and possible outcome to the story.

Second half of the Midpoint — At the 50% - 52.5% mark, Romanoff cooly turns the tables on Loki, revealing her vulnerability was really a TRAP at the first-half Midpoint to gain needed information. Armed with new insight into the enemy's plans and strengths (Q&A), the S.H.I.E.L.D. team debates their next move. But in a twist on the LOVE VS. GOAL beat that's uniquely appropriate for an ensemble story, rivalries and insecurities threaten to splinter the team's united loyalty apart, distracting them from an ATTACK closing in quickly on their blindside.

The Giver, by Lois Lowry

As the protagonist advances along the path of internal growth, he may grow apart or distant from friends and allies who continue to embrace the status quo of Act One. The lessons he learns along the way separate him from the pack, even if he continues his daily life side-by-side with them. By the Midpoint, he comes to understand he knows too much to go back to the way things were before.

First half of the Midpoint — At the 47.5% - 50% mark, The Giver imparts memories of sky and sunshine to Jonas. They are so pleasant, he wonders at being warned about pain. So The Giver enables him to experience sunburn, a tiny GLIMPSE of the unimaginable and deeper pain yet to come. Back at home with his family and friends, Jonas realizes that more than professional duty prevents his sharing his new memories. He's CUT OFF by his family and friends' fundamental lack of understanding. How can he find words to give another the experience of sunshine?

Second half of the Midpoint — At the 50% - 52.5% mark, he sees more and more things "differently," such as his friend's hair, but he doesn't know what it means. After some Q&A, The Giver confirms Jonas is beginning to see the color red, and will eventually see the world in all its manifold colors. This new awareness not only changes the protagonist's perception of the story world, but the reader's, as well.

Laura (1944)

Genre affects which plot threads step into the spotlight at key turning points. In the earlier examples from Vera Caspary's mystery novel, the Midpoint directly addressed the protagonist's investigative efforts to solve the case. The movie adaptation elevated the importance of the romance, and it shows in the key turning points. It's worth noting that in both versions (as in all mysteries) the murderer puts in a clue-worthy appearance at the Midpoint without attracting suspicion.

First half of the Midpoint — At the 47.5% - 50% mark, homicide detective Mark McPherson makes himself at home late at night in Laura's empty apartment, searching through her personal things for a GLIMPSE into her life and the mystery surrounding her death. He keeps returning to gaze at her portrait over the fireplace mantel.

Second half of the Midpoint — At the 50% - 52.5% mark, the murderer arrives and attempts bargaining with Mark for a clock he wants released from the crime scene. Waldo knows Mark wants the portrait of Laura over the mantel for himself, and taunts him: "Have you ever dreamed of Laura as your wife?... I see you have... You better watch out, McPherson, or you'll end up in a psychiatric ward. I don't think they've ever had a patient who fell in love with a corpse." (LOVE VS. GOAL: the protagonist's obsession with Laura conflicts with his investigation.) Mark gets rid of Waldo and falls asleep in a chair, staring dreamily at Laura's portrait. When he awakes to find Laura's returned from the grave, it seems Waldo's prediction has come true.

Once Upon a Time. Season one, episode twelve, "Skin Deep."

This episode retells "Beauty and the Beast" with Rumplestiltskin as the protagonist emotionally-crippled by cowardice, and Belle as the love-interest/antagonist who challenges him to change. In a unique twist, it's the antagonist rather than the protagonist who tries to quit the story at the Midpoint, but is Cut Off by the villain disguised as an ally.

First half of the Midpoint — At the 47.5% - 50% mark, the Evil Queen Regina's carriage overtakes Belle on the road as the young woman escapes her indentured life with Rumplestiltskin. Although

Belle GLIMPSES the love she has in her heart for Rumple, she can't go back because "something evil has taken root in him." Pretending to be her friend, Regina CUTS OFF Belle's flight by encouraging her that any curse can be broken by true love's kiss.

Second half of the Midpoint — At the 50% - 52.5% mark, Belle decides to give the relationship another chance. (LOVE VS. GOAL) Rumple watches from his castle's tower for her return, and is as overjoyed as a schoolboy when he sees her coming, though he tries in vain to adopt an unconcerned mask. Belle peppers him relentlessly about missing her: "Admit it! You're happy I'm back." (Q&A) Finally, she breaks him down into bashfully confessing: "I'm not *unhappy*."

Princess of Mars, by Edgar Rice Burroughs

Discovering a chance at love is a reliable and powerful way to raise the stakes and make them intensely personal, especially if that discovery immediately precedes the threat of danger. Instantly, there's more at risk. While the backstory revealed here belongs to a supporting character instead of the protagonist or love interest, it nevertheless portends a possibly tragic ending for star-crossed lovers such as Carter and Dejah Thoris in a world built upon punishing love and killing hope.

First half of the Midpoint — At the 47.5% - 50% mark, John Carter regains consciousness to find himself injured and his attacker slain. Dejah Thoris, believing Carter dead, is overcome with grief. Her cold indifference to him was the result of injured pride, and he GLIMPSES the tender truth of how deeply she cares for him.

Second half of the Midpoint — At the 50% - 52.5% mark, the Thark woman Sola reveals to Carter the secret of her parents' ill-fated love affair, the name of their betrayer, and the identity of her father: "I know that I can trust you, and because the knowledge may someday help you or him or Dejah Thoris or myself... My father's name is Tars Tarkas." (Q&A)

Seed of Evil, by David Thompson

A character may be Cut Off from an important ally at the Midpoint only to discover an unforeseen ally willing to pitch in and help. Often in such a case, the ally brings with him unexpected resources, such as knowledge the protagonist didn't realize before he needed, or special skills that may fill in specific areas where the protagonist lacks abilities.

First half of the Midpoint — At the 47.5% - 50% mark, Chases Rabbits is near his goal of finding Nate King and bringing him back to the trading post, when he learns the legendary frontiersman is not at home. (CUT OFF) Nate's son, Zach, interprets the message Chases Rabbits delivers to mean the Crow maidens working at the post are in danger (GLIMPSE of higher stakes), and returns with the anxious young warrior to render aid.

Second half of the Midpoint — At the 50% - 52.5% mark, the Crow maidens reach the limits of their patience waiting to begin the sewing work they agreed to do at the trading post, and question their employer. (Q&A) The answers they get are shocking and terrifying. They have been tricked there under false pretenses. The men intend to pimp them out for money. When the Crow maidens try to leave, they discover they are prisoners with no way to ESCAPE.

Winds of War, by Herman Wouk

This sweeping epic of World War II follows a large cast of characters swept up on the turbulent tide of global events. Most Midpoints are stronger for focusing their limited space on only one or two beats.

However, at well over 360,000 words, this novel has ample room to develop and explore multiple beats capturing not only a significant turning point in the war, but in the relationships of its central characters, the Henry family.

First half of the Midpoint — At the 47.5% - 50% mark, US Naval intelligence observer Pug Henry stands beside young Englishwoman Pamela Tudsbury on her patio "watching the Luftwaffe start its effort to bomb London to its knees." At first it appears to not do much damage, but a closer GLIMPSE reveals an ugly and painful preview of the blitz to come. Invited by Churchill to be an observer on a RAF bombing ATTACK over Berlin, Pug gets an up-close-and-personal GLIMPSE of the British air campaign and his own mortality when the plane is hit and nearly goes down. He returns exhausted, but alive and well to Pamela's passionate welcome. Feeling like he's "stumbling through dreams within dreams," he GLIMPSES what a tenderly intimate life with Pamela might be like. Despite temptation, Pug remains faithful to his absent wife, but realizes he's fallen hopelessly in love.

Second half of the Midpoint — At the 50% - 52.5% mark, Pug receives orders returning him promptly to the US via Berlin. Trapped between LOVE VS. GOAL, Pug shares an awkward, miserable goodbye with Pamela. Back at home, his wife slips into adultery with another man. "Like a declaration of war, it drew a line across the past and started another era." A proposal of marriage confronts her with her own LOVE VS. GOAL, and she finds herself reluctant to jettison twenty-five years with Pug for a new relationship that may sour with time. Meanwhile, Pug is entertained by Berlin big shots at a weird weekend getaway full of Q & A about his observations of the British war effort and German assertions of inevitable victory.

Welcome to Temptation, by Jennifer Crusie.

Even when the protagonist is willing to put himself at risk for his goal or an important relationship, well-intentioned allies may disagree and try to boot him out of the story for his own good. Their concern for someone they care about simultaneously reinforces reader empathy for the protagonist, while also sharpening the point to the stakes. It isn't only up to the protagonist to be paranoid about consequences. Other characters believe in them, too, and probably know where the bodies are buried to prove it.

First half of the Midpoint — At the 47.5% - 50% mark, Sophie's overprotective brother tries in vain to CUT OFF her relationship with Phin, concerned it's a repeat of her high school heartbreak. He and her sister accurately GLIMPSE she's in love with Temptation's "town boy" mayor, and remind her of painful backstory to drive home the stakes involved. (True GLIMPSE of backstory plays double-duty as a false GLIMPSE of possible negative future outcome to the romance.)

Second half of the Midpoint — At the 50% - 52.5% mark, Phin's domineering mother makes a surprise ATTACK against him on the city counsel, fueled by her determination to drive Sophie out of town. Concerned for his future, she demands he break up with "that woman," but Phin tells her firmly and lovingly to back off. When it comes to LOVE VS. GOAL, he wants his chance at love. Meanwhile, his motherless daughter pays a surprise visit to Sophie to find out if she's suitable mother material. (Q & A)

Conclusion

The scarlet fuse sizzles to the quick. The tightly twisted bow tying it to the bomb ignites in a flash of sparks.

The protagonist's face blanches white as a sun-scorched skull.

You dive for cover behind a mossy bolder. A concussive roar of fire and shrapnel blasts the rock like a dry hurricane. The explosion shreds the protagonist's false beliefs, pulverizes his old self-defeating ways of behavior, and lays bare his values to the bone.

Peeking through your fingers, you spot a figure hurled like driftwood through the seething dust and flames. It's your protagonist! Bloody and obviously in considerable pain, he stumbles but regains his footing. Without a backward glance, he races out of the Great Swampy Middle as though a congregation of hungry alligators were snapping at his heels.

You hang onto your Indiana Jones-style fedora and hurry after him. "Hey, wait for me!"

With the explosive central tension of the Midpoint propelling the writer and protagonist forward into the second half of the story, all brakes are off. Pacing almost takes care of itself as the writer rapidly unwinds the remainder of the fuse to the third key tension event at the break into Act Three.

This sprint out of the dark heart of the Everglades strips the protagonist of the last and most closely cherished of his old support systems. When the antagonist strikes again, it makes the protagonist's fear real to him as never before. Just when he's ready to give up or thinks he can avoid the antagonist by keeping his head down, the fuse ignites another explosive event in the plot. He's forced to cast his lot wholly with the thematic virtue and decide upon a New Direction that, while seemingly suicidal, eventually brings him (and readers) to a satisfying conclusion.

Which is the happiest kind of ending for the writer. Arriving on dry land, it's time to kick off your waders, pop open a root beer, and toast your surviving and thriving in the Great Swampy Middle!

Once you've mastered the two-part Midpoint, the Everglades of Act Two will never again drown a good story in dangerous quicksand. Following the scarlet cord from tension point to tension point becomes at the same time easier and more unique with each successive story as your interpretive imagination gains confidence.

Instead of a journey filled with dread and discouragement, the Great Swampy Middle becomes a thrilling land of discovery and anticipation. Let the adventure begin!

Texts Cited

Ackerman, Angela, & Puglisi, Becca. *The Negative Trait Thesaurus: A Writer's Guide to Character Attributes.* JADD Pubishing, 2013. Print.

Alessandra, Pilar. *The Coffee Break Screenwriter.* Studio City: Michael Wiese Productions, 2010. Print.

Appel, Wendy. *InsideOut Enneagram: The Game-Changing Guide for Leaders.* San Rafael: Palma Publishing, 2011. Print.

Bell, James Scott. "The Magical Midpoint." *The Kill Zone: Insider perspectives from today's hottest thriller and mystery writers.* Clare Langley-Hawthorne, Jodie Renner, Kathryn Lilley, PJ Parrish, Joe Moore, Nancy Cohen, Jordan Dane, Elaine Viets, Joe Hartlaub, Mark Alpert, & James Scott Bell. July 7, 2013. Web. January 10, 2014.

Brooks, Larry. *Story Engineering: Mastering the 6 Core Competencies of Successful Writing.* Cincinnati: Writer's Digest Books, 2011. Print.

Butcher, Jim. LiveJournal blogpost dated July 11, 2006. Web. October 18, 2013.

Crusie, Jennifer. "Questionable: Conflict in Romance." *Argh Ink.* Jennifer Crusie. January 31, 2014. Web. March 17, 2014.

Decker, Dan. *Anatomy of a Screenplay: Writing the American Screenplay from Character Structure to Convergence.* Chicago: The Screenwriters Group, 1998. Print.

Edson, Eric. *The Story Solution: 23 Actions All Great Heroes Must Take.* Studio City: Michael Wiese Productions, 2011. Print.

Field, Syd. *The Screenwriter's Workbook: Exercises and Step-by-Step Instruction for Creating a Successful Screenplay.* New York: Dell Publishing, 1984. Print.

Gulino, Paul Joseph. *Screenwriting: The Sequence Approach.* New York: The Continuum International Publishing Group Inc., 2004. Print

Howard, David. *How to Build a Great Screenplay: A Master Class in Storytelling for Film.* New York: St. Martin's Press, 2004. Print.

Hudson, Kim. *The Virgin's Promise: Writing Stories of Feminine Creative, Spiritual and Sexual Awakening.* Studio City: Michael Wiese Productions, 2009. Print.

King, Vicki. *How to Write a Movie in 21 Days: The Inner Movie Method.* New York: Harper & Row Publishers, 1988. Print.

Maass, Donald. *Writing the Breakout Novel: Insider Advice for Taking Your Fiction to the Next Level.* Cincinnati: Writer's Digest Books, 2001. Print.

Mernit, Billy. *Writing the Romantic Comedy: The Art and Craft of Writing Screenplays That Sell.* New York: HarperCollins Publishers, Inc., 2000. Print.

Riso, Don Richard, with Hudson, Russ. *Personality Types: Using the Enneagram for Self-Discovery.* New York: Houghton Mifflin Company, 1996. Print.

Riso, Don Richard, with Hudson, Russ. *The Wisdom of the Enneagram: The Complete Guide to Psychological and Spiritual Growth for the Nine Personality Types.* New York: Bantam Books, 1999. Print.

Seger, Linda. *Making a Good Script Great.* 2nd ed. Revised & expanded. Hollywood: Samuel French Trade, 1987, 1994. Print.

Sheppard, Lynette. *The Everyday Enneagram: A Personality Map for Enhancing Your Work, Love, and Life... Every Day.* Petaluma: Nine Points Press, 2000. Print.

Snyder, Blake. *Save the Cat Strikes Back! More Trouble for Screenwriters to Get into... and Out Of.* Saline: Save the Cat! Press, 2009. Print.

Snyder, Blake. *Save the Cat! The Last Book on Screenwriting You'll Ever Need.* Studio City: Michael Wiese Productions, 2005. Print.

Snyder, Blake. "Midpoint—The Key to Cracking Any Story." *2012.ScriptFrenzy.org.* 2008. Web. February 12, 2014.

Swain, Dwight V. *Techniques of the Selling Writer.* Norman: University of Oklahoma Press. 1965.

Vogler, Christopher. *The Writer's Journey: Mythic Structure for Writers.* 2nd ed. Studio City: Michael Wiese Productions, 1998. Print.

Vorhaus, John. *The Comic Toolbox: How to Be Funny Even if You're Not.* Beverly Hills: Silman-James Press, 1994. Print.

Wheat, Carolyn. *How to Write Killer Fiction: the Funhouse of Mystery & the Roller Coaster of Suspense.* Santa Barbara: John Daniel & Company, 2003. Print.

Williams, Stanley D.. *The Moral Premise: Harnessing Virtue & Vice for Box Office Success.* Studio City: Michael Wiese Productions, 2006. Print.

"Glimpse"

of her ~~in~~ the before

the garage?

did the view bring

back focus, she wasn't

in the picture really.

SET READERS FREE TO *FEEL* YOUR STORY

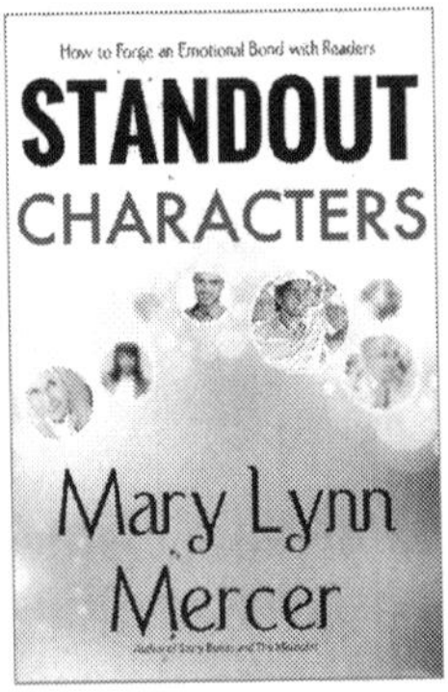

Remember the favorite stories on your "keeper shelf," and more than likely the first thing that pops vividly to mind are the characters. That's because truly great stories make readers *feel*, and standout characters are the primary key to unlocking those emotions.

To lose themselves in a story, readers need to be given rooting interests in the characters they're spending time and money on. Rooting interests are developed from specific physical, moral, and psychological traits that emotionally bond readers to the character. Spicing page after page with these empathy traits in fresh and imaginative ways puts the writer in control of readers' emotions like working tumblers in a lock.

Take your writing to the next level by learning how to deliver the kind of fantastic emotional experiences readers crave. This book empowers you to craft your story with the reader in mind, and capture their hearts with exciting and emotionally involving characters. You'll learn–

- How to lay the foundation for standout characters by using quick and simple characterization tools to create a working snapshot.
- The one indispensable trait every character must have that's essential to winning readers' empathy.
- Three different categories of rooting interests and how each works to evoke specific emotional responses in readers.
- Which empathy traits work best for which kinds of characters, and the special circumstances that can permit a character to get away with almost anything.
- How to use flaws to bond your protagonist closer to readers, and create villains readers love to hate.
- How to skillfully combine traits to effectively illustrate your theme while still fulfilling genre conventions and satisfying readers' expectations.
- Quick tips from analyses of the seven most iconic heroes, heroines, and villains ever to come alive on the page or screen.

2 A

6 1 Dixie Gala - year-end 7 trade
the Watch (questions)

2 [illegible]

3 Missing [illegible] Bride [illegible]
[illegible] [illegible]

4 [illegible]

5 [illegible]

8 [illegible]

9 [illegible]

0 [illegible]

31,000

52
15,62000
15,5000
161,2000

$\frac{.50}{31100} = \frac{.52}{x}$

52x =

$\frac{60}{1.24}$ 3/1 . 12400 / 62400

12400

12400
3
37200

744 0 0

31,000
2)62000

2 A

6 1 Free Julie - you can't handle the truth (foreshadow)
2 Calls Dylan
3 Mimi gets closet visit | Lenke answers Dylan went off

7 (1) Annie let me meet you somewhere
(2) Tells Camden Julie not with LV
3

Stakes: Reputation, Legacy

8 Closet visit
1 Woman calls, saw brooch in ad — brooch not there
2 Another woman calls, her brooch originally
3 Did Mimi / Willow take brooch ? because

9 1
2
3

10 Midpoint - Annie dies ?"
Amy - pregnant

2 B

"I'll show him the photo. He'll understand with the ..." (to Dylan) to page

~~Mimi~~ Julie tries to talk Annie out of sale

Maybe it's not meant to be.

Camden! I can help you with this? Would ~~Mimi~~ Julie indulge in revealing Annie desire

Did ~~Mimi~~ Julie tell Mimi anything about gossip picked up

Mimi hears sale "going" to Annie

Made in the USA
Middletown, DE
09 April 2015